QUAKER SAILORS

U of P and the U.S. Navy

The V-12 at Penn in World War 11

Robert B. Hamilton Jr.

1995

HAMILTON BOOKS

Division of Hamilton Publishing
P.O. Box 94
Montoursville, PA 17754-0094

HAMILTON PUBLISHING
P.O. Box 94
Montoursville, PA 17754-0094

Library of Congress Cataloging-in-Publication Data
        Catalogue Number: 95-94809
        Hamilton, Robert B., Jr.
Quaker Sailors/Robert B. Hamilton Jr.

Quaker Sailors/UofP and the U.S. Navy
The V-12 at Penn in WWII

        ISBN   0-9648802-0-2

Other By Author:

"Changing Course at Fredericksburg"
"Navy UDTs in WWII"
"From Fisher's Pond to Sagami Wan"

        Printed in the U. S. A.
Jostens Book Manufacturing

CONTENTS

PREFACE

"With broken heart, and with head bowed in sadness,
but not in shame, I report..... that today I must
arrange terms for the surrender of the fortified
islands of Manila Bay...., Corregidor....,
Fort Hughes...., Fort Drum...., and......."
(message faded away).......
                Lieutenant General Jonathan M. Wainwright, USA
                Last message from Corregidor 06 May 1942

Such were General Wainwright's last words as a free man until flown directly from a POW Camp in Manchuria in September 1945. And, arriving just in time to stand behind General MacArthur, and along the side of General Sir Arthur Percival, the British officer who had relinquished Singapore in 1942, he would vindicate his almost four lost years on the deck of the Missouri at the September 2nd surrender ceremony in Tokyo Bay.

With similar messages almost commonplace..... confidently certain that "the" day would come... , the only reaction that Americans could permit themselves was to... grind their teeth...., bite off a lip.... , kick their dog.... , or somebody's dog.... , try to keep a dry eye.... , and be patient!.

And the long road back.... , a road across a much wider Pacific than today .. , would require a Navy that had never been envisioned by the most dedicated Naval expansionist.

After over 20 years of public apathy, which manifested itself in numerous isolationist groups, and in spite of all of the Navy's proud posturing, they continued to work with old worn out hardware. About all it had to fight with, would be the fortitude of the fighting men who would bring the Navy back from it's position behind the "goal line".

Inspiring the young men that followed, the officers and men of those early operations fought an awesome war. And as a result of the compelling accounts, as spelled out in the action reports of ships lost, new recruits "joining up" gave considerable thought to how far they could swim... , how long they could last... , stay afloat... , in a wintry sea.

Faced with two wars to fight on hundreds of fronts, suddenly there was a desperate need for thousands of junior officers to man the most formidable fleet that will ever exist. With no time to permit an education on the scale of the Naval Academy, BuPers's call was for patient young men who could sustain a condensed "crash" academic and Naval Science curriculum.

The Navy had already accomplished a major step forward in it's recruiting task years earlier when many of their future officer candidates were only "picture show" loving kids.

All during the 1930's, the Fleet, which at the time was "home ported" in San Diego, was often used by Hollywood to shoot scenes off the California Coast while at the same time successfully glamourizing itself. And had repeatedly aroused a soft spot for "bellbottoms" among that "Great Depression" generation. Films like, "The Fleets In", and "Don't Give Up the Ship", with Dick Powell singing the title song. And others had Wallace Breary usually playing a convincing old CPO with a uniform sleeve lined with gold "hashmarks". Jimmy Cagney, who played the part of the Admiral, and who worked directly with Halsey, to produce "The Gallant Hours", (Halsey's screen biography), often played Navy and Marine parts along with his Irish sidekick, Pat O'Brien. Often depicted as "leathernecks", it didn't hurt the Marines in their recruiting successes a few years hence. Even the news reels, such as "Fox Movietone News", would continuously run a film trailer showing the Navy's Battleline, all 15 of the 35,000 ton Battleships, plunging through "green water" in the Pacific preparing for any eventuality with the publicly conceded devious Japanese.

And while Navy "gobs" were often depicted as leading a carefree sailor's life, the young actor officers, in Navy blue and gold, were serious heroes whose deeds would unfailingly capture the desire of the pretty movie heroine. And why not? With deep California tans, set off by crisp high white collars, and gold bars on their epaulets, in the parlance of the times, those Navy "whites" were "lady killers"!

Of course there had to be higher levels of calling than the ones just described. But it's not difficult to concede that it was very rare to find a Navy Man...., of any rate or rank..., who had not stood a little taller when wearing "Navy Blue".

In many ways the University had been relegated to carrying on in a barely passive supporting fashion. Only peripherally involved in many of the aspects of the Navy's program, there were those at Penn that barely understood what was taking place around them.

Initially considered specifically as a series of anecdotes illustrative of that period permitting the illumination of a tiny vignette of the University's wartime history, "Quaker Sailors" was not intended to assert a personal experience or point of view. Merely to shed some light on a unique period and, uncertain of wider interest, to reignite a little nostalgia for those affiliated with Penn during that period. And for those living U of P alumni, albeit they are in their 70s now.., and playing in their last quarter, it's almost certain that there will never again be such a group in the history of Penn.

Having shed their uniforms quickly at the war's end, racing to make up for lost time and to get on with their lives, they left just as rapidly while leaving little record of that interval of time at Penn. Objectively scrutinized after a half century, as with a multitude of other conventions in American life, those years of continuous dramatic historic events can not help, but also, remain unique in the University's history.

As a group, V-12s have subjectively minimized their initial selection.. , their varied duty in the Navy after being commissioned.. , and their wide range of pursuits as civilians subsequent to being awarded their degrees.

Now..., after over 50 years .. , but not as with a class, and seen as a specific cohesive unit (V-12s are scattered among probably as many as six to eight classes)... , little consideration has been given to record that period of the University's involvement with those "teen aged" Navy Officer candidates.

While a few former Penn Sailors continue to meet regularly to recollect with old friends, other schools hold small reunions.. . Still others, because of distances, find a variety of ways to continue long range friendships.

And there are those with only fading recollections. Even they occasionally find a reason to repeat a yarn or two of amusing personal experiences.

Much has been hashed over concerning the academic advantage provided those V-12 officer candidates. But the truth of the matter is, the Navy's earlier attempts to fill it's officer requirements through it's V-7 officer recruiting program had been found wanting. Without math, physics, engineering drawing, and other basic college required courses, the qualifications of too many of those officers were limited in scope. This led to a variety of complications which narrowed their ability to adapt to their shipboard duties. The Navy could easily find and commission administrators; but the urgent need was for "Line" Officers. Those commissioned at one of the three Midshipman Schools, after completing V-12 training, enjoyed an indisputable reputation for being well prepared for their assignments. The Navy, the schools involved, and sailors combined to make the program an outstanding success.

CHAPTER I.

"Admiral Turner Had To Know"

"Although the planning by BuPers to meet the needs of the new "two ocean" Navy was superb, it was impossible to predict transformations in the evolvement of amphibious warfare. And it wasn't flawless. The Navy relied heavily on V-12 Officers to help to meet those unanticipated requirements."

By February 1943, the Joint Army Navy Board had done its work and completed its selections. And the University had been notified that it had been selected by Navy for a V-12 Unit. When the final tally was complete, 130 other colleges and universities had also been selected, a total of 131.. .

Although eager to cooperate with the Navy, with which it had excellent experience in a number of other programs, at the time of notification, it had not been fully concluded as to how the University would be compensated.

In 1942, when the Joint Army Navy Board was established, its purpose was to negotiate the necessary arrangements with each of the 131 participating colleges and universities. Many of the terms of the contracts with the V-12 Schools were derived from those of the similar arrangements made earlier with the Midshipmen Schools, Columbia, Notre Dame, and Northwestern. And references included the V-5 pre-flight schools such as those at Penn and the University of North Carolina at Chapel Hill.

By June, the conditions had been established and negotiations, to determine the methods in which to compensate the participating colleges and universities, were nearing completion.

A.) Physical Education Instructors were to be furnished by the Navy to administer the Navy's own program under the overall direction of Commander Gene Tunney. A monthly facilities fee was paid for each trainee.

B.) Cost of special equipment or facilities, or modification of equipment or facilities, for the Navy's special requirements were to be borne by the Navy.

C.) Building use compensation was uniform and all institutions were paid the same; 4% of "book value"

D.) Converting the Palestra into a "Mess hall', the food operation was contracted to "Horn and Hardart".

E.) Tuition was based upon that charged civilian students.

The Commonwealth of Pennsylvania and State of New York, both with nine (including New York's Webb Institute of Naval Architecture), had the most schools in the program. They were followed by Ohio with eight, California had seven, and Massachusetts was in fifth place with six. Alabama, Arizona, Arkansas, Missouri, West Virginia, Oregon, Oklahoma, Maine, New Mexico and Florida, each with one, had the fewest.

Pennsylvania, represented disproportionately, by both the number of it's youth in the Armed Forces and the overwhelming contribution of it's major heavily diversified industry to America at war, once again led the way in lending support to the Navy's Officer candidate needs. And nine schools, from among the best of the Commonwealth's colleges and universities, were selected by the Navy:

Ursinus College	Collegeville. PA
Penn State College	State College, PA
Franklin and Marshall College	Lancaster. PA
Villanova College	Villanova, PA
Bucknell University	Lewisburg, PA
University of Pennsylvania	Philadelphia, PA
Muhlenberg College	Allentown, PA
Bloomsburg State Teachers	Bloomsburg, PA
Swarthmore College	Swarthmore, PA

Although in 1942, only Penn, Brown, Harvard and Yale had NROTC units on their campus, all eight of the Ivy League Schools were selected early on by the Department of the Navy. Already in use as one of the Midshipman Schools, all but Columbia University provided for the "basic" trainee program. The Marine Corps had placed units on four "Ivy" campuses; Cornell, Dartmouth, Princeton, and Yale. For Engineering "majors", the Navy selected Brown, Columbia, Cornell, Penn and Yale. And all eight of the "Ivy" schools qualified to provide the Navy with a Pre-Medical and Pre- Dental curriculum.

At Penn, Medical School and Dental School V-12s were furnished subsistence and allowed to make their own living arrangements. Although classified as V-12s, and Apprentice Seamen, they were furnished with Midshipman uniforms. Not being a part of the V-12 Battalion, they were not required to muster, make any of the formations, take calisthenics, or study any of the usually required math, physics, engineering or Naval Science courses.

And by the middle of 1944, BuPers came to recognize that by late 1945 they would have accomplished what they had set out to do. Early in 1945... , even before "VE" Day... , the Department of the Navy had planned for all, and in some instances were beginning negotiations, of the schools to conclude the program. Having supplied the numbers of officers sufficient to meet the fleet's expansion requirements, predicated on the experience to date, and completion of those already selected, the individual commands would be either consolidated or terminated.

To emphasize it's prestige and to show their support for the officer candidate program, both the Secretary of the Navy and the Undersecretary made numerous visits to V-12 campuses. Secretary of the Navy, Frank Knox, as well as his successor, then Undersecretary, James V. Forrestal, were trustees for a V-12 school. Knox for Michigan's Alma College and Forrestal for his alma mater, Princeton University in New Jersey. Forrestal added a personal viewpoint in that he had experienced a similar Navy program during the First World War.

The everyday oversight of the program had been assumed by Vice Admiral Jacob's Assistant Bupers Chief, Rear Admiral Louis E. Denfeld.

In one of his early Congressional appearances, Secretary Knox would testify that the Navy should plan for a war that would extend into 1946-47. Later, the War Department indicated their logistical planning was for the conflict to continue through 1949-50. In terms of fleet expansion, the Navy Department had projected that the "build up" would not "wind up" until 1950.

A Republican in a Democrat Administration, Henry Knox was the Secretary of the Navy from 1937 until 1944; through the period of the beginning of the transformation into a U.S. Navy with effective "two Ocean" fighting capability, through the dark aftermath of Pearl Harbor, and the historic "turning point" when the Jap Fleet was devastated at Midway.

Knox was succeeded by James Forrestal, who held the office of Secretary of the Navy, from May 19, 1944 through 1947. When he was succeeded by John L. Sullivan, in that post, Forrestal was appointed by President Harry S. Truman to become the first Secretary of Defense. Forrestal held that office until 1949.

According to friends, Forrestal had decided, even before the end of WWII, not to go back to Dillon, Read and Company, where he had succeeded Clarence Dillon as president of the firm in 1938. Had he lived, it has frequently been asserted that he could have been Dwight Eisenhower's opponent in 1952. It is firmly understood that consideration had a great bearing on his acceptance of the post of Secretary of Defense.

Almost immediately after taking office, it was the new Secretary of the Navy, James Forrestal, who awarded and signed the commissions of my class at the U.S.N.R. Midshipman School at the University of Notre Dame.

Although the planning by BuPers to meet the needs of the new "two ocean" Navy was superb, it was impossible to predict transformations in the evolvement of amphibious warfare. And it wasn't flawless. The Navy relied heavily on it's V-12 Officers to meet those anticipated requirements.

In the late Summer of 1944, Admiral Richmond Kelly "Terrible" Turner, Commander Amphibious Forces Pacific, had turned his attention to the year ahead; to the long contemplated invasion of the Japanese homeland. Turner's plan anticipated that the "top secret" UDTs would play a powerful role. With orders to report to Admiral Chester Nimitz's Pacific Headquarters at Pearl Harbor, he released Commander Draper L. Kauffman from his Command of Underwater Demolition Team 5. Upon arrival, Kauffman was told by Admiral Turner that his immediate assignment was to work on UDT plans for the invasions of Yap, Palau and the Phillipines.

Kauffman also learned soon after arriving at the Pacific Command Headquarters that he had been assigned a dual staff role. Selected by Kelly Turner for the job as Turner's UDT plans officer, as such, that duty would cause him to spend a lot of his time with the Admiral's staff at Pearl. Also during the same period, in his other role as UDT Training Officer, he continued to shuttle to the UDT'S top secret training base on the leeward side of Maui. Over on Maui Kauffman had the good fortune to be supported by a top notch staff headed up by Commander Jack Koehler, Executive Officer to Captain Ajax Couble, Commander of the Maui Base.

Koehler had come to the Pacific Theater from the ETO and done a masterful job of running one of the first UDT operations for Admiral Turner... , the invasion of Kwajalein. In the 1950s, capable Jack Koehler would again be called to serve his country and become Assistant Secretary of the Navy in the Eisenhower administration.

As "plans officer" for Turner, Kauffman became, for the first time, privy to some of the secret future operations already in the planning stage. From these meetings he received his first indication of the details of the operational plans to invade Japan. And he was surprised to hear that the tentative date discussed was within the year.

Made somewhat uneasy by the thought that the UDT operation could well be largely his responsibility, his main concern centered around the recognition that, if the projected plan were to be carried out, the existing force fell far short of the requirements that Kauffman knew would be needed. He knew he had to act fast. From the meager data available for his consideration, he decided to place an estimated requirement of thirty teams which he believed necessary to carry out operation "Olympic".. , the invasion of Kyushu. And "Coronet".. , the invasion of Honshu. Having experienced first hand the capabilities of the Fort Pierce training facilities, his first consideration was it's inability to meet those training requirements. He proposed that the training capacity at the Florida base be "beefed up" immediately. It needed to be tripled... , and fast! He conveyed that critical assessment to Admiral Turner who promptly approved the recommendation. Both Kauffman and Turner knew that would require a special sailor... , only volunteers.. , both enlisted and commissioned... , for "extra hazardous duty". At Kauffman's urging, the Admiral sent communiques classified, "Urgent", to Bupers beseeching the immediate need to expand the training capacity in Florida. And the Admiral had to know!

In fact both Turner and Kauffman speculated that, should the controversial operations against Formosa and China be the chosen route to Japan, it may be necessary to by-pass Fort Pierce and expedite training for immediate operations through the tiny secret base on the leeward shore of Maui.

Ordered to report to the Philippines shortly after the Okinawa landings..., Commander Kauffman reported to Manila for duty at MacArthur's Headquarters with the staff of the Eighth Army's General Eichelberger. With time running out, the UDT Commander gave all of his time to planning the invasion of the Japanese home islands. An expansion of the planning initiated months earlier when assigned to Kelly Turner's Staff at Admiral Nimitz's Headquarters.

Upon arrival at Manila, Kauffman was almost immediately confronted by firm and unanticipated opposition to his UDT plans. It wasn't the details of the plans... , Eichelberger's Staff objected to the general role of the UDTs in the invasion operations.

It was O.K., according to the Army's viewpoint, for the Navy to make the pre-invasion reconnaissance, and to clear the way for the Navy and Marine Corps operations. The U.S. Army would supply it's own Amphibious Combat Engineers to clear the beaches in advance of their own troop landings.

Having observed the "Teams" in action... , in the water and on the beaches at Guam, Saipan, and Okinawa... , the senior Combat Engineer, a veteran Army General, promptly accepted the reality that the formidable conditioning required of the UDTs gave them a "lock' on that type of operation. Not within the competence of his Amphibious Engineers, he came out strongly in support of

Kauffman and the "top secret" UDTs. In retrospect, the UDT skipper reasoned, the General may not have wanted to debate the issue with the irrefutable "Terrible" Turner. With his reputation of a fierce temper and obstinate personality, Turner was proclaimed the winner of many an argument...., even without confrontation.

Still, the Army was deeply concerned with the expectation that the Japanese planned to use innovative and extreme measures to repel the initial assault by "Olympic" and "Coronet" invasion forces. Reports of gasoline ready to be piped to invasion beaches were common knowledge to Pacific forces. Not refuted by September 2nd, those reports were not dispelled until UDTS made a reconnaissance of Japanese beaches.

Although Kauffman gradually secured the endorsement of the other "Flag" Commanders, Turner's early foresight, to seize upon Kauffman's recommendations and lend his powerful understanding and unwaivering support, was instrumental.

Recognizing the need to tighten the timetable, in his capacity as the UDT Plans Officer to General Eichelberger's staff, Kauffman went "flank speed' ahead planning Operation "Olympic" and "Coronet" . He would quietly concede that the magnitude and potential cost in casualties of those operations brought about a privately contained personal pessimism for the first time. And years later, would concede that it had been his first experience of encountering a mood of depression concerning the war.

The initial operation against the Southern most island of Kyushu was ordained for late October or early in November 1945. Kauffman would later reason, "it seems to me that the best we could hope for was to lose two-thirds of our people". Believed more difficult than the coast of France, acceptable landing opportunities were limited. And also, because experience led them to understand that the Japanese would be more fanatical than ever in defending the beaches of their home islands. "Olympic" called for three landing areas to which ten teams would be assigned. At the outset Kauffman planned to use the initial three teams, those to be replaced with the second three teams and finally those three teams to be also replaced with even three more teams. The first six Teams were expected to sustain casualties to the extent that they could no longer function as cohesive units. It was Kauffman's plan to hold the remaining 10th Team in reserve and available to insert should the attack become bogged down.

Not confined to Kauffman alone, in the viewpoint of Eichelberger's Staff, the pessimism that he felt was pervasive. Recalling that particular period of victory demonstrations, of the secession of the war in the European Theater, there were indications of general despondency. Probably a morose, traceable to the

beginning transition to peacetime life by others, causing subliminal feelings of doubt by those left out of them. And facing an
uncertain future in the Pacific.

Along with others, with first hand experience from that era,
UDTs would forever remain convinced that dropping the two
nuclear bombs had saved many lives on both sides. Japanese
casualties would have been tremendous..., far exceeding the
number lost as the result of dropping those two bombs.., on
Hiroshima and Nagasaki.

Although there would be no civilian casualties for the Americans, with logistics and amphibious operations believed to exceed
those complications faced at Normandie, military losses could be
comparable to those of the Japanese defenders. And, as with that
of other Commanders faced with the assignment of sending their
men into Operation "Olympic" and "Coronet", the morality of
dropping the bomb was never an issue with UDTs.

Several months into their curriculum, the former V-12s, matriculating at the United States Navy Midshipman School at the
University of Notre Dame, began to speculate about the assignment they would draw several weeks prior to being commissioned. In the course of a very thorough training and indoctrination, they would have an opportunity.., in general terms.., to
specify preferences and priorities of interest in those assignments... . Individually they would envision their choice of duty...,
Destroyers, Cruisers, Battleships, Submarines.. , and all the
stereotypes that they had come to know. Duty that had been
impressed on them by some of their battle experienced instructors and likewise by other fleet experienced Midshipmen.

But without prior explanation, by their Company Officer, one
hot humid late Indiana summer day... , on all "decks".. in the
"dorms", the Midshipmen.. were discussing the abrupt appearance of a request for "volunteers" for a "top secret... extra
hazardous duty" assignment. The obscure bulletin board announcement and request specified "volunteers", in such a way,
that it captured the imagination. Stressing, "must be in top
physical condition.. , capable of top secret and dangerous operations", the tiny notice provided spaces for the names of only a few
volunteers. Instigating further intrigue, the urgency was exemplified by the need to make a decision to "sign up" within 48 hours.
Out at Pearl Harbor, the UDT Command had to know!! Time was
of the essence, the "Olympic" and "Coronet" UDTs had to be in the
"pipeline".. . Turner could not wait. He had to know!!

As would be expected, the bulletin immediately sparked lots of
discussion and speculation among the Midshipmen. But after a
few initial gestures of bravado, and posturing conversation, still
no one ventured forth to sign their name in any of the spaces

provided for that purpose for the first twenty four hours.

Titillated with the idea of "secret and extra hazardous duty", but not anxious to show an extraordinary interest, I resisted a strong impulse to sign my name. Quietly confiding in an old roommate and V-12 classmate from Penn... , billeted in a room immediately adjacent to mine on the fourth floor of old Walsh Hall, we began to talk about it. Attracted to the siren call of an adventurous assignment, with little discussion... , late that night we became the first two Midshipmen in Walsh Hall to sign the sheet. The first step to an interview.

Not bothering to tell me, just before the names were picked up by the Battalion Officer... , my ex-roommate changed his mind and removed his name. Surprised not to find his name among those scheduled to be interviewed, I began the "one on one" conferences and testing on my own. The ex-roommate ultimately became the "skipper" of an "LCT".

Beginning with an early morning interview with a very young Lieutenant Commander Eacho.. , my interest and enthusiasm to be accepted into the "special duty" assignment grew immediately. The Commander's purposely vague description of the tentative assignment, and especially the potential for early action, permitted plenty of room for the imagination. After lengthy training and waiting, just what I knew I needed. Presenting an impressive appearance, obviously chosen with considerable forethought, his deep tan, set off by a stark white shirt with it's starched stiff detached collar against his Navy dress blues, was further enhanced by 2 1/2 stripes of gold. And the familiar "blue and gold" was further accented by a chest full of "fruit salad".. .

It was a hot humid Summer day in Indiana.. , Staff Officers of the Midshipman School were dressed in pants and shirts.., "khakis" and "grays". No doubt about it, BuPers had a handle on recruiting! More than a few Midshipman were " dress blues" inspired that day.

Commander Eacho was never seen or heard of again..., not at Fort Pierce.. , not at Maui... , not with any Team.. , not on any APD... , not at Coronado.. . No doubt about it, BuPers had a handle on recruiting!

Almost immediately, BuPers passed the word that there was no longer a need for "Scouts and Raiders". Instead, another urgent request from the Pacific Command for volunteers for what came to be known as "Underwater Demolition Teams"...., "UDTS". With not a lot of prompting to accept the change, the Navy did a careful job of quietly "plugging" the UDTs.. It would be years before the timing of the Navy's stance would be understood. And what had taken place.

Reacting immediately to the direct and urgent communique of

the forceful Pacific Amphibious Forces Chief, Commander Eacho was dispatched by BuPers to South Bend within a matter of hours. With responsibility for the success of anticipated amphibious operations of unprecedented magnitude, Turner had underlined the need for Underwater Demolition Teams. The need was urgent.. , and he assigned it "top priority". With that action, having already convinced Bupers they had no strategic mission or similar urgency, Turner effectively wiped out the "Scouts and Raiders".

And that Commander Eacho seriously alluded that Congress was contemplating a bill to grant "extra hazardous duty pay".. , same as submarine duty... , of fifty percent, did not escape those volunteering at Notre Dame. "Extra pay" sounded good, elevated the volunteers enthusiasm, and certainly did nothing to detract from their interest.

Especially well conducted interviews with Commander Eacho concluded on a very positive and upbeat note when he arranged for the anticipated further testing. This particular battery of tests included... "I.Q." and psychological in both written and oral form. And Eacho wrote orders for strength and swimming testing to be given at familiar Knute Rockne Gym the following day. Records of Midshipman "physicals" and "strength tests", almost a daily event since arriving at Notre Dame, apparently were not deemed acceptable to meet "UDT" standards. Several days after Eacho returned to Washington, physicals were the order of the day.

Told to sleep on it, to consider a decision that night, those interviewed agreed among themselves that not a lot had been learned. Discussions or answering questions of inquisitive roommates as well as other Midshipmen, had been discouraged by Eacho. Rationalizing the recruiter's interviews with other candidates only generated more enthusiasm for the assignment... , and a few became more committed. And even in the early interviews with Commander Eacho, it was stressed that the door to "pull out" was always wide open... Permissible to withdraw without prejudice at any point.

Volunteers would not hear a word on their interview, or on the testing, until a week before graduating and accepting a commission. Those chosen were relieved to learn of their acceptance. Other Midshipmen, not notified of their duty until the night before graduation, had not even been interviewed for their choice of duty. "Cut" at BuPers, the Midshipmen having submitted and ranked their choices weeks earlier, new officer assignments were sent to South Bend for distribution after the graduation ceremony in the new Navy Drill hall next to the Notre Dame stadium. Upon taking the oath, the just commissioned UDT Ensigns, all former V-12s, went back to their billets to pick up orders instructing them to proceed individually and report to the "Amphib" base at Fort Pierce. Mimeographed orders stated "to report to Fort Pierce, Florida, and to the Commanding Officer, Amphibious Training Base, for temporary duty under instruction in a Combat Demolition Unit." Signed by Vice Admiral Randall Jacobs, Chief of the Bureau of Naval Personnel, the instructions specified that travel was to be by public transportation to be reimbursed at USNATB, Fort Pierce, Florida.

Never having been further South than Washington's Mount Vernon home while on a family vacation to the District of Columbia, Florida evoked images of a remote sparsely settled subtropical mix of swamps, beaches, ocean and jungle... , sprinkled with a few remote Winter resorts. And that is exactly the way that it was!

The U.S.N.R. Midshipman School at Notre Dame would train another three classes of mostly V-12s.

And with the war in Europe at an end, and those forces available to the Pacific, by July 1945, the role of the U.S.N.R. Midshipman Schools had become inessential. Ordered to shut down forthwith, the V-12s would no longer avail themselves the opportunity of attending one of those schools to earn a commission.

Having contributed slightly fewer than 60,000 physically capable and professionally trained junior officers, the Navy's V-12 program had performed exactly in the manner in which the Navy had intended it.

CHAPTER II.

"Pacifist Warriors"

"But a dilemma, of the War Department, was to find a way to fill the anticipated demand for junior officers required to fill an already rapidly expanding "two ocean" Navy. And particularly irking to Americans was the implication, sometimes even a prediction, that the war would prevail... , over their lives.... , for unforeseeable years into the future. Though Americans were resolutely optimistic... , still... , these were ominous and dangerous times! And others, mixed with their optimism, were just plain damn mad as hell!"

Arriving at night after a two day trip by rail, surrounded by swamp, dense jungle, and ocean, the remote "NCDU" camp was a sanctuary of primitive darkness. Standing around about a half hour, and very warm in "dress blues", even the ocean breeze was getting warmer... Prospects for a quick cold shower and a bunk were not encouraging. While the "OOD" rousted out a base Storekeeper 2nd to hustle up some bedding, not finding any chairs, I sat down on the only seat available... , my seabag. The "OOD" was talkative and, as is almost always inevitable, he began talking about his duty before having been sent to this remote and primitive island base off the coast from Fort Pierce between the Indian River and the Atlantic. A young well tanned "j.g.", comfortable in "greens" and helmet liner, walked in and, overhearing our exchange, interjected, "Penn Quakers.. Huh!! How `bout that? I thought Quakers were pacifists?? What's a 'U of P' Man doing down here with the "Shootn', Fightn', Dynamitn' Demolitionaires??" Sticking out his hand, "I'm John Horrocks."

Not the first time that I had heard that. The Quaker pacifist comparison, lightly alluded to on a number of occasions at Penn by V-12s from the mid-West, also appeared to spark questions from those Notre Dame Midshipmen from the South and the West.

As the fourth class to graduate from Notre Dame, the Midshipmen were from all over the country. From Georgia, the "Dawgs", from Penn State, home of the "Nittany Lions", from up in New Hampshire came a few Dartmouth "Indians", and right there in that bastion of Indiana football, the "Fight'n Irish" of Notre Dame.

And even one of my roommates, who ran with me up and down those four flights of stairs a dozen times a day to the fourth deck of old Walsh Hall, was a Yale "Bulldog".

It may be a little understandable that a university, that refers to itself as the "Penn Quakers", might just attract a little "flak" from schools with names like "Warriors", "Gators", "Tigers", "Panthers", and "Longhorns". Anyway, this "pacifist" did not hit the sack right after that introduction. With about 80 other newly arrived men and officers, at about 2200, we were marched down to the beach for a little night indoctrination. Half mile out and half mile back.., and wound up the evening by crawling over the "dune line" "sneak and peek" style, across 300 yards of brush and sand "moguls", to be checked off by a waiting member of the training staff. And we finally did get fed! After a few sandwiches and pitchers of ice tea in the "mess" tent, we finally located our tents and bunks well after midnite.

One Hundred and thirty one colleges and universities answered the urgent call of the United States Navy in World War Two. Their assignment... , "to utilize their institutions to give direction to the training of a select group of officer candidates needed to man the massive fleet expansion underway." While 125,000 men were enrolled in the schools over the three years of the program's existence (no more than 70,000 at a time), less than sixty thousand actually completed the program.

Fifty years after our Team had been decommissioned in November 1945 at Coronado Island, and going our separate ways, I met with two former UDTs from my old outfit.. , one of the early Navy Underwater Demolition Teams.., (now Navy Seals). Reminiscing, while feasting and enjoying a freshly killed venison dinner cooked by a former bos'n mate at his hunting camp deep in a remote rural area of Pennsylvania's woods, one of the ex-UDTs semi-chided, "weren't you a 90 day wonder?" Never having had a reason to discuss and compare our service time prior to our first meeting in Florida back in the forties, both had been under the impression for all those years that I had entered the Navy only a few months before coming together at the Fort Pierce NCDU Base. Not so! I had been a sailor for almost two years before we battled our way through the classified UDT training and the now infamous "Hell Week". For those who survived it, sharing that experience would earn the other's esteem and affection in a manner which will remain unshaken.

I readily recall milling around on the parade ground one early dark morning before muster in front of "headquarters" tent. And overhearing an enlisted sailor asking, "did you get a look at those fucking officers... ?" Half of them don't even shave!" That was a little too much... , for me. With all hands in "jungle greens" and helmet liners, no rank identification, I could confront the boisterous "sea lawyer", and did, "since when do you judge a man by his beard?"

Exposed to some pretty substantial responsibility, many V-12s were just nineteen years of age when Secretary of the Navy James Forrestal signed their commission. Returning to the states shortly after my twenty first birthday, many nights I would find myself to be the ranking officer on duty at the Fifth Naval District Shore Patrol Headquarters on Court Street when there were more than one hundred thousand sailors, assigned to the newly forming "Atlantic Fleet", pitching liberty in downtown Norfolk.... Most of them on Monticello Avenue and Granby Street. And hanging out at the "Monticello Roof", on the top of the hotel by the same name... , officers tried to hide their enlisted "Wave" dates at curfew knowing full well that all enlisted personnel had been directed by the Commandant of the 5th Naval District to have returned to the Norfolk Base. Although the hotel's "house detectives" were all over the place, no one ever claimed that they were successful in making certain that there was no "hanky panky" at the Monticello.

But many of those on liberty did their drinking at the "Krazy Kat", where the favorite sport of sailors was fighting each other with broken beer bottles. Happening to be in Norfolk on business for The Atlantic Refining Company for a day or two in the Summer of 1960, the city had just initiated an urban renewal project. And was in the process of relocating businesses and tearing down a lot of old buildings. The legendary "Krazy Kat" was about to capitulate to the "wreckers ball". And that night..., the headline in the Norfolk newspaper read, "Sailors Around the World Mourn the Passing of the Krazy Kat." Being a sentimental guy.. , even that event could bring on pangs of remorse.

U.S. forces were still on the defensive and the war was not going well for the Allies in the Fall of '42. The outcome of the Guadalcanal operation, a "seesaw" campaign, continued to be in "limbo". And bleak reports of Allied losses... , frequently precipitating unspoken pessimism and uncertainty, were met by Americans with unresponsive stoic resolve. Momentarily.., the "Axis".., the three powers... Germany, Italy, and Japan, were invincible.

But a dilemma, of the War Department, was to find a way to fill the anticipated demand for junior officers required to fill an already rapidly expanding "two ocean" Navy.

And particularly irking to Americans, was the implication, sometimes even a prediction, that the war would prevail.. , over their lives... , for unforeseeable years into the future.

Though Americans were resolutely optimistic... , still... , these were ominous and dangerous times! Others, mixed in their optimism, were just plain damn mad as hell!

As FDR, an ex-Secretary of the Navy, and his own administration's Navy Secretary, Frank Knox, proceeded with their massive plan to build up of the fleet, it became very clear that the Navy's traditional officer source could not possibly satisfy the rapidly increasing requirements. The V-1 (college program for freshmen and sophomores), and the V-7 (college juniors, seniors, and recent college graduates recruited to the inactive reserve) programs held out little hope of meeting a fighting wartime Navy's officer personnel requirements. Having already been enlisted, these men remained in college in the "inactive reserve" waiting to be called to active duty.

By January 1943, mandated by an order from FDR in December 1942, the program was defined and initiated by Rear Admiral Louis E. Denfield, USN, then an Assistant Chief of Naval Personnel. With the solid endorsement of Vice Admiral Randall Jacobs, the Chief of Naval Personnel over at BuPers, he ordered the program to be executed within six months... , by July 1, 1943.

Already one of the twenty seven colleges and universities in the country with an ROTC unit, Penn had existed for over two centuries along side the United States Navy in the old port city of Philadelphia. With it's many Naval persuasions and traditions, Penn was truly a Navy school.

Early on the morning of Thursday July 1st, 1943, with all 784 thoroughly tested and screened, the selected V-12s (including activated ROTCs), converged on the corner of 34th and Spruce..., Irvine Auditorium. Such was the suddenness of the "mess hall" conversion of the Palestra, and the arrangements with "Horn and Hardart", that they had not completed setting up. And no one would be fed until late that evening. And frequently there were those, having taken all day and evening to be processed and assigned quarters, who weren't issued bedding until well after midnite. Although it had been a long day, a Chief Specialist (A) made the rounds announcing that "all hands" would muster for "chow formation" in the "big quad" at 0700! And Chief Jack Stevenson was there!!

For men in Penn's NROTC, and those others who had already been enrolled at Penn, after a few weeks at home, it was merely a return to the campus. But, now that they were on active duty as Apprentice Seamen, their status would be the same as that of any other raw recruit.

Other V-1 and V-7 Reserves, waiting for months to be placed in an "active duty" status, their future governed by the needs of the service as prescribed by BuPers, also reported on July 1st.

And effective July 1, 1943 through June 30, 1946, the N.R.O.T.C. would accept only applications from within a V-12 unit. With most Penn sailors unwilling to trade their "bell bottoms" for N.R.O.T.C. dress blues, there were few "takers" at Penn.

Congratulating the new Navy Men on their selection on the

basis of ability and aptitude, when Commanding Officer L.M. Stevens, Captain USN (Ret.) addressed the Battalion, he emphasized the Navy's urgent need "to further a continuing supply of qualified officer candidates in the various fields required by the U.S. Navy, Marine Corps and Coast Guard."

A diversity of sailors had been assigned to Penn from colleges and universities from across the country. From the University of California at Berkley, Michigan, Northwestern, Wisconsin, Rutgers, VPI, Madison Jr. College, University of Virginia, Temple, University of North Carolina at Chapel Hill, Penn State, Purdue, Amherst, Cornell, UCLA, Dartmouth, etc. Most had traveled all the prior night or nights to time their arrival as stated in their orders..., Thursday morning. Having been assigned from ships far out in the Pacific, it had taken several almost a month to reach Philadelphia. It took most of the day for a few stragglers to find 34th Street after their trains finally pulled in to either the Broad Street or Thirtieth Street station. Those few arriving early..., a day or two ahead of time.., found a reasonable room and an intriguing introduction to West Philadelphia at the nearby Hotel Normandie.

But for the most part, both Penn and the Navy, had prepared well for their new arrivals. To serve as a "Ships store" and supply warehouse, only days before the Navy had completed a frame building at the back of the "Big Quad". Manned by Navy "Storekeepers", the hurriedly assembled structure served as storage for bedding and uniforms to outfit all, including the NROTC. Although also holding the rank of Apprentice Seaman, it was finally ruled that the NROTC would retain their same "midshipman style" uniforms.

All those V-12s assigned to Penn on that Thursday morning in July 1943 were issued a comprehensive booklet entitled, "Regulations for Trainees". A sampling of only a few of those covenants are as follows;

Section II of the regulations described the organization of the unit:

201. Administrative Section The Commanding Officer of the unit will be the Professor of Naval Science and Tactics, University of Pennsylvania, with offices in 311 Engineering Building.

The Executive Officer, who will be directly responsible for the administration of the program, will have offices at Weightman Hall.

202. Medical Section will be administered by a commissioned

medical officer and staff with offices in Foerderer House.

203.   Physical Training Section with a commissioned officer in charge assisted by a staff of Chief Specialists (A) will have offices in the Hutchinson Gymnasium. 204. Disbursing Section will be administered by a Disbursing Officer with staff in Weightman Hall.

Section IV   "Standing Orders and Regulations" gave the number one spot to and emphasized:

A.   Academic
401.   Attendance at classes. Students must attend all regularly scheduled classes unless excused by the Executive Officer of the V-12 Program.

402.   Conduct during classes. During classes, students will sit erect and conduct themselves in a military manner. No student shall leave the classroom during the class period unless properly authorized.

403.   Failures. Failure to pass one or more required courses in a single term may result in the disenrollment of a student, upon which he will be ordered to general duty in an enlisted status.

404.   Procedure to and from classes. The varied academic program in effect will not permit the marching of students to and from classes. Students will, however, conduct themselves in a military manner proceeding to and from classes, taking the most direct route and when engaged in conversation, it will be in a quiet manner.

405.   Smoking. Smoking will not be permitted on the campus, the street, or in the classrooms, washrooms, or corridors of instruction building.

A few other of the pertinent orders were;

408.   Bunks, lounging on. Students will remain clear of bunks except during recreation and liberty periods.

412.   Neatness of Rooms. From 0730 to 1600, Monday through Friday inclusive, and from 0730 to 1200 on Saturday, rooms will be ready for inspection. The following will be observed:
        (a) Rooms will be swept out.
        (b) Bunks properly made.

    (c)   Clothing and equipment neatly stowed.
    (d)   Decks, bulkheads, furniture, waste baskets, and ash trays clean.
    (e)   No photographs, banners, etc. hung or posted on bulkheads

419.   Telephone messages. Students should inform friends that they cannot be reached by telephone except in cases of extreme emergency.

425.   Automobiles. Students shall not have automobiles available for their use while at the university.

429.   Eating on street. Students shall not eat while on the street or campus.

435.   Leave. No leave will be granted except in cases of urgent necessity.

440.   Mustaches. No mustaches, beards, or sideburns shall be worn.

444.   Uniform of the day. The uniform of the day will be established by the Commanding Officer in conformity with the seasonal uniform set by The Commandant of the Fourth Naval District. Students will be in prescribed uniform at all times other than during athletics or when in their rooms.

There was a whole section entitled "Military Conduct and Courtesies". It charged the trainees with the proper Naval conduct in addressing their officers.. They were to answer a question with a "Yes Sir" or "No Sir". The reply "Very well, Sir" or "Very good, is made by a senior to a junior, but never by a junior to a senior.

And there was a substantial eight paragraphs on saluting including,

449 (h).   Saluting In the presence of women out of doors, caps should not be removed. To acknowledge their presence on first meeting, students should salute.

452.   Women in public. Students shall not show undue signs of affection when walking, standing, or seated in public with women.

Section V was entitled, Discipline

501.   <u>Demerits</u>.

(a) Demerits will be assigned for the first offense for the following infractions in amounts indicated. Subsequent offenses of a similar character will be assigned demerits in such amounts as the Executive Officer of the V-12 Program may consider <u>necessary</u> under the circumstances.

		Demerits
1.	Smoking or eating in street	5
2.	Failure to salute superior officer	5
3.	Failure to stand at attention when addressed by a superior officer or when being addressed	5
4.	Out of uniform	5
5.	Untidy in dress or appearance	2
6.	Lounging in unauthorized places	2
7.	Unnecessary noise	2
8.	Drinking at unauthorized place or time	50
9.	Intoxicated or drunken condition-subject to disciplinary action	10
10.	Unbecoming conduct	10
11.	Damage to property—pay damages	25
12.	Tardiness at drill, classes or formations	2
13.	Late returning from liberty or leave	15
14.	Going beyond liberty bounds	25
15.	Disrespect	25
16.	Talking in ranks	5
17.	Riding automobiles at unauthorized time	10
18.	Gambling	25
19.	Possession or use of firearms	25
20.	Unmilitary bearing	3
21.	In unauthorized places	20
22.	Failure to obey orders	15
23.	Non-possession of Demerit or N. NAV. 546 I.D. card	5
24.	Not observing rules for study hours	5
25.	Absence from drills, classes, and formation without authority	10

(b) When a student has received an aggregate of demerits as follows:

First Term	150 per term
Second term	100 per term
Third term	75 per term

he shall be called before the Commanding Officer.

502.   <u>Demerit Cards</u>. Demerit cards which will fit in the jumper pocket will be carried by students at all times. Each student should write his name on all cards. These will be given to an officer at his request when an in- fraction of regulations is noted.

505.   <u>Further Disciplinary Action</u>. Separation from the Naval Training Unit because of misconduct may also subject the offender to further disciplinary action, courts martial, or separation from the service.

<u>Section VI</u> under "General Information"

601.   <u>Achievement Examinations</u>, prescribed by the Bureau of Naval Personnel, will be given at the end of the first two terms and at such other times as the Commanding Officer may deem necessary to check on the progress of students.

608.   <u>Religious Observance</u>. No religious facilities are furnished on this campus by the Navy. There are, however, adequate facilities for those of all faiths in the vicinity and students are urged to attend religious services. Information may be obtained by consulting the Saturday editions of the local newspapers.

609.   <u>Sick Call</u>. Sick call will be held in the Naval Medical Department, Foerderer Hall, at the following hours:

          0700   0830   1130   1730

610.   <u>Uniforms and Equipment</u>
   (a) The following items of clothing in the quantities indicated will be issued gratuitously to students who were not previously issued full bags:

Quantity	Item
1	Broom, whisk
1	Brush, shoe
4 pr.	Drawers, nainsook
12	Handkerchiefs
1 pr.	Leggings
1 pr.	Overshoes
2 pr	Shoes, black, low
1 pr.	Shoes, gymnasium
4 pr.	Sox, cotton, black
2 pr.	Sox, wool, natural
3	Towels, large
1	Trunks, bathing
4	Undershirts, cotton

(b) In addition, the following items will be issued as a temporary loan:

Quantity	Item
1	Cap, blue w/ribbon
1	Cap, watch
1 pr.	Gloves, woolen
3	Hats, white
1	Jumper, dress, blue
2	Jumper, undress, blue
3	Jumper, undress white
1	Jersey
1	Neckerchief
1	Overcoat
1	Raincoat
2 pr.	Trousers, blue
4 pr.	Trousers, white

Appendix "A": provided for procedures and precautions in the event of Air Raid drills.

Appendix "B": provided extensive instructions in the event of a fire.

Appendix "C": detailed comprehensive instruction to the "stu dent security watch".

Appendix "D": outlined extended "Instructions to the house captains", whose tour of duty extended "from 0800 Monday until 0800 the following Monday. The house captains will be on duty 24 hours per day and will be accessible at all times when not at classes or meals.

Among his duties, to insure that his men were responding to reveille, out in the A.M. for calisthenics, tours of inspections with an officer, widows etc. secured in the event of a storm, report to the O.O.D. breakages or needed repairs, not allow civilians in the dorm except as authorized, report anyone planning to be absent from a meal, all lights to be extinguished by 2215, deliver the mail twice daily, posting notices, handling liberty requests, etc.

For the next several days.. , and over the weekend, the Philadelphia Inquirer .. , and the Bulletin.. , covered the changes made by the Navy program on the West Philadelphia campus.. , at Villanova.. , and at Swarthmore. With numerous articles appearing on various aspects of the transition taking place in West Philadelphia, apparently the most intriguing to covering reporters was the conversion of the Palestra into a "mess hall".

A headline in the July 1st issue of the "Philadelphia Inquirer" announced............... ,

"Navy Trainees Arrive Here Today for Study".

It indicated that about 260 of that group, from Allegheny and Pittsburg counties, would arrive as a delegation to attend

Swarthmore, Villanova, and Penn. Trainees from the Philadelphia area would climb aboard that same train at Thirtieth Street Station bound for Princeton, Columbia, Stevens Institute of Technology, Brown, and Yale.

Another Inquire headline read...................... ,

"Mess Hall Cancels Sports in Palestra"

"The Palestra, famed University of Pennsylvania indoor sports arena, will become a mess hall for Army and navy trainees at the University beginning tomorrow.

The huge hall, which has a seating capacity of 10,000 and is one of the largest of it's type in the east, has already been converted into a cafeteria for the use of various service units now stationed at the University.

1612 Seat Set Up

The cafeteria will be operated for the University by the Horn and Hardart Baking Company, operators of a chain of restaurants, cafeterias and automats in this city.

When it goes into operation at breakfast today, 184 tables, with seats for 1612 men, will be available in the center of the main floor under the north and south balconies, with space remaining under the north balcony for additional seats if they are needed.

100 To Feed Trainees

Complete kitchen equipment has been set up under the east and west balconies, for the use of approximately 100 civilian employees, who will feed the trainees from eight service counters at the rate of 20 men a minute for each counter.

Conversion of the Palestra into a wartime dining room will mean that all indoor sports contests of the University which were formerly held there will be transferred to gymnasiums and other buildings elsewhere on campus, it was learned last night. No further contests will be held in the Palestra for the present.

Hugh Floor Space

The first floor now being used for a cafeteria covers nearly 16,000 square feet, including 7150 square feet in the basketball court. Men using the hall for meals will enter by two ramps on the east end................................ .... The Palestra, which is near Franklin Field and adjoins Hutchinson Gymnasium, on the Pennsylvania campus, was formally opened January 1, 1927 with a Yale-Pennsylvania basketball game........................ ...."

Obviously the big news that week end in Philadelphia was the conversion of the Palestra!

But it didn't take long for the big gymnasium to loose it's "locker room" aura.... . It quickly became a three times a day magnet for hungry Penn Sailors. And most of whom would develop a robust appetite for "H and H's truly Philadelphia cooking.

CHAPTER III.

"...Where The Hell Did All These Sailors Come From?"

"Those seeking a "Deck" or "Line" Officer Classification would learn their trade at Midshipman School. With its strictly Navy curriculum, that included courses in Navigation, Naval Ordinance, Seamanship, Communications, Damage Control, Recognition, Ship Handling etc., these men graduated as "seagoing" professionals."

For most destined for the newly commissioned Naval training unit at Penn, "reporting on board", a phrasing with which they were about to become familiar, meant only a days travel. Others, from as far away as California, and even a few from Fleet forces in the South Pacific, had come a much longer distance. Traveling sometimes almost a week on crowded railroad coaches, they crossed the country along with thousands of other service people on the move to bases and ships around America at war. As often the case with thousands of other servicemen and women in that busy time of wartime assignments, many had spent the prior night sleeping on trains or in railroad stations along their route to Penn.

If they had some prior briefing, the future Penn Men traveling by train got off at Philadelphia's Thirtieth Street Station. Those not getting directions in advance usually found themselves at the end of the line in the cavernous Victorian era Broad Street Station. Having come only the last few miles by electric diesel, these men had spent most of the time on dirty coal fired steam trains with little sleep or food. Limited by the Navy to those 17 to 20 years of age, the arriving young officer candidates were mostly interested in getting a shower and finding some breakfast. They were grateful for the shower that finally came late that night after a busy first day of orientation and "getting settled in" activities had run their course. From now on the United States Navy would make all the big decisions..., even when you could have a shower.

For those riding in packed coaches, a trip to the dining car could mean losing their seat. Instead, the lunch menu, dispensed by a white coated vendor walking the aisle with a large "hamper", was limited to dry sandwiches selling for a dollar... Not a paltry sum in the forties. Coffee and milk, freshly replenished at stations along the way, was available on a first served basis until quickly sold out.

The "almost" Penn Men found both Philadelphia stations bustling with more activity than ever recorded by the Pennsylvania Railroad before or since World War II. Looking forward to breakfast, and in a hurry to disembark, inevitably led the soon to be sailors to their first encounter with a Horn and Hardart. In 1943 there were numerous "H & H's" in, and around, the city to feed hungry Philadelphians at a very reasonable price. For those getting off at 30th street, the nearest "H and H", directly across from the station on Market, became a regular stop in the months ahead for Penn sailors returning from leave or liberty. Those remaining on board until the end of the line would get off at the massive Broad Street Station located at the East end of the infamous Market Street "Chinese Wall". From there it was only a short walk to several "H & H's", including one of the restaurant company's world renown "automats".

The South Broad Street "H and H" cafeteria, only a few steps South of Chestnut, and a brisk walk from the Broad Street Station, became a mid-town favorite. Relatively new, it was located within sight of City Hall and opposite the Academy of Music. Attracting all types of service men with a few hours to pass, including many foreign sailors from the ships of U.S. Allies, a popular authentic "Stage Door Canteen" was easily accessible in the lower level of the nearby Academy.

About to become an intimate part of their daily life, frequently Penn Sailors would gain their first experience with that much maligned Philadelphia institution from one of those Horn and Hardardts. After establishing the "Mess" in the Palestra, Penn's famed indoor sports arena with a seating capacity of 10,000, the Navy chose "H an H" to operate the "galley". Although it had been formally opened 16 years earlier with a Penn-Yale basketball game on January 1, 1927, in 1943, the University took pride in the fact that it continued to invoke national prominence. Virtually abandoned, due to increasingly severe war time restrictions, it permitted the Navy to make use of that big and usually noisy place by converting it's use to feed it's young officer candidates. Palestra food would readily be conceded by Philadelphian's to be vintage Horn and Hardart fare. And you either liked it, even becoming defensive of it, or, as with a few, complained about it incessantly for the rest of the assigned time at Penn. But others, myself included, became "H and H" fans for life.. , and even miss it... . And sometimes, nostalgically exaggerating it's virtue... , elevate it to a level above that of "home cooking".

Orders were specific in designating a "reporting time" of 0900 on Thursday July 1, 1943. While the future Penn Men were making their way to Philadelphia, far out in the South Pacific on that same day, General MacArthur was finally beginning a minor offensive against the Jap held Rendova Island. Standing off Rendova ready to wrest the remote jungle island from the Japs, Australian and American Naval forces were prepared to land troops early on the morning of the 2nd. And the "Nips" were in for a lot of trouble! America, the sleeping industrial giant, finally aroused and showing the first signs of a long brewing whiplash eruption, was about to embark on defining the destiny of the Axis Powers for the next century.

For weeks the city had been experiencing sweltering Summer heat reminiscent of the mid 1930s. And this day was predicted to be more of the same... , a clear, but oppressive, sticky hot, and humid Philadelphia July day. The heavy humidity was not helped by the smoggy and smelly pollution pumped out by some of Americas most strategic heavy industries, rendering plants, soap processors and refineries working around the clock in South and Southwest Philadelphia to support the war effort. The multitude of bituminous fired industry furnaces, as well as coal fired steam locomotives shuttling their boxcars and gondolas to every point in the city, contributed to the smothering haze and heat that sought the lower levels over the Delaware Valley and West Philadelphia Penn campus. With the exception of a cold shower, none of those in the University's ageing non-air conditioned buildings could anticipate any relief. And the sun had been long out of sight before the new sailors were permitted any kind of relaxation in the old brick dorms. 1940's air conditioning was limited to a number of the better downtown theaters, including those, like the massive and relatively new Mastbaum at Market and 19th. Where Penn sailors occasionally welcomed a cool break from the Summer heat.

As early as 0730, early arrivals, most still in civilian clothes, began to congregate and mingle on the Irvine common. Meeting for the first time, often it meant an evolvement into a life time of friendship. Instructed in their individual orders to report by 0900, the men had been arriving at the appointed location..., 34th and Spruce... , well in advance of that deadline. By 0900, the sun had burned off the lingering morning haze.. , and you knew that it would be sweltering hot the entire day. While early arrivals had formed a queue, and were unprotected near Irvine's entrance, late appearing Penn Men gathered in small groups in the shade and sat around on the low brick retaining walls along the streets..., both 34th and Spruce.

Irvine, with it's high spire and massive brick edifice, was most likely selected to receive the new Penn Navy men because of it's high visibility, and easy to find location, at the Northwest corner of 34th and Spruce.

All of the architectural anecdotes concerning Irvine, related by seeming "anxious to relate the story" returning Penn students..., "old timers"... , surfaced like a depth charged submarine. By 1000, most of the new hands were familiar with simplifications of the engineering debacle concerning the acoustics, or lack of them, in this architecturally controversial recent addition to the Penn Campus.

Irvine had been designed by the firm of Horace Trumbauer, a well known Philadelphian. Having also designed the Free library of Philadelphia, the Racquet Club, and the Widener mansions in Elkins Park, the Trumbauer firm was also one of two employed to design the Philadelphia Museum of Art.

Built for the American Sesquicentennial held in Philadelphia in 1926, the Curtis Organ, the world's largest, had been relegated to a home in Irvine. On that hot July 1st day, the University's organist welcomed the new sailors and periodically helped to lighten the confusion with a medley of military and patriotic war tunes. And was given rousing encouragement by all hands when the organ's thundering pipes let go with a spirited rendition of "Anchor's Aweigh".

Built to resemble Mont St. Michel, off the Northwestern coast of France, Irvine rises 200 feet above ground level. Part of the Irvine lore.... , attributes the controversial auditorium's design, by it's donor, as "revenge" for reportedly having been "flunked out" of the School of Architecture.

V-12 sailors had been accepted to Penn that July morning with many different educational histories. High Schools and Prep Schools were sending their outstanding June graduates, some having graduated within a few days prior to July 1st. Very young men, they had successfully weathered the battery of testing originated by a specially created officer recruiting unit. In 1941 and 1942 volunteer college men across the U.S. had successfully worked their way through the Navy's selection process.. , and having been passed by it's Review Board, accepted in the V-1, V-5, and V-7 Officer Candidate Programs. Having been alerted earlier by the Navy to anticipate "orders", many put their life on hold for many months expecting earlier assignments to active duty. Others, with several years of college under their belts, had expected to go directly to one of the three Reserve Midshipman Schools. And they were not pleased to find that they faced additional math, physics, and engineering courses in order to become eligible.

Still in their "teens", those young men converging on Penn's Irvine Auditorium that July morning had seen their youth somewhat inhibited by the extremes of the "great depression" era in which they had grown up. Though thin, some even downright skinny... , most were physically hard .... And ripe for the training upon which they were about to embark.

To accommodate the need, to man the many new ships of the rapidly expanding multi-ocean fleet with sufficiently trained officers, the Navy had created U.S.N.R. Midshipman Schools. Making it possible to earn a commission, the three schools were located on the campuses of outstanding major Universities. Operated by the Navy, with their own curriculum and officer instructors, the facilities were provided by Northwestern University at Evanston, Illinois, Columbia University in New York City, and the University of Notre Dame at South Bend, Indiana. Fortunate to spend a hot and humid Indiana Summer studying at Notre Dame, the reward was a commission as an Navy Ensign..., a "Line" Officer... . And I came away with a warm and lasting fondness for that school.

Already in uniform, when presenting their orders to a Navy Yeoman at Irvine on that hot July 1st, a few of those reporting came directly from other duty posts scattered around the world. Extremely proud of testing successfully, prouder even to have been sent from the Fleet, their application had required an extremely strong endorsement from their Commanding Officers. A few came from bases within the country, even directly from "boot camp".

With a first hand grasp of Navy life, the few sailors, sent ashore from the Fleet, shared their experience with others. Having been assigned to Penn directly from the South Pacific, one Kansas sailor had not been aware that the story of his ship had not been made public. And on one occasion, out of the "blue", when an unrelated Wharton subject was the topic of conversation, he abruptly switched to, "Ham, you never heard about the Boise?" His demeanor would indicate he wasn't just jesting. And I did a lot of listening! For security reasons, the Cruiser Boise's outstanding battle history had apparently been withheld. Following it's policy of not providing "aid and comfort to the enemy", the Navy did not release the complete story until months later.

The "Light Cruiser" Boise had been commissioned in Philadelphia on December 3, 1936. Similar to other ships of her class and vintage, she had an approximate displacement of 10,000 tons, a beam of 69 1/2 feet, her length at the water line was 600 feet, and had storage for 2100 tons of fuel oil. With a complement of approximately 1100 men and officers, she had an armament of 15 six inch deck guns, some twelve 20 and 40 MMs, plus eight 5 inch 25 calibre to provide anti-aircraft firepower.

In October 1942, with the Guadalcanal campaign still in doubt, she was attached to a Fifth Fleet force comprised of Heavy Cruisers San Francisco and Salt Lake City, the Light Cruisers

Helena and Boise, and the Destroyers Duncan, McCalla, Farenholt, Buchanan, and Laffey. The Boise force tangled with the "Tokyo Express", also comprised of cruisers and destroyers, off Cape Esperance at the Northern tip of Guadalcanal, just before midnight on October 11th.

"Blacked out", and fighting in darkness, both sides blasted away non stop for approximately forty five minutes. The gun fire was hot.. , rapid, and furious by both sides. Each a small force, they were about evenly matched.

Having surprised the Japs, the Boise force quickly sank a heavy cruiser and a destroyer. Hit many times by U.S. gunners, another "Nip" heavy cruiser barely managed to sneak away in the dark. Although, a much needed morale building American victory, it wasn't a disaster for the Japs. And it did not come without a price! Boise had been hit and badly damaged; Destroyer Duncan had been sunk.

Earlier that year, shortly after "Pearl Harbor", the light Cruiser Boise had seen some action with the Asiatic Fleet Strike Force under the overall Command of Admiral Thomas C. Hart. Traversing the Flores Sea, East of Java and South of the Celebs and Borneo, Boise's English language charts proved to be inaccurate. While the Dutch could supply better charts, they claimed that they had no pilots available to read them in their language. The Boise's Navigator was obviously having his difficulties. The result being that Boise ripped her bottom wide open while the S-36, a submarine commanded by John R. McKnight, ran hard aground on a coral reef.

S-36, the first submarine lost during the war due to grounding, had been proceeding to Soerabaja, Java, when she ran up on Taka Bakang reef in Makassar Strait. Underway at standard speed, with strong and difficult to predict currents in that area, a low tide covered the reef. Her forward battery compartment flooded, the alarmed McKnight sent out an uncoded request for assistance.

Nearing Soerabaja, Sargo turned back to assist. Not willing to risk another sub, the South Pacific Submarine Commander ordered her to terminate the rescue effort. Instead, a PBY was dispatched to obtain help from the Dutch. Unable to rock her free, and enemy forces moving closer, the entire crew of the S-36 was safely removed before she had to be abandoned. A Dutch ship, S.S. Siberote, came to the rescue and all hands were saved. Prior to abandoning, McKnight ordered S-36 to be rigged to flood at high tide.

With overworked and tired crews, shortages of fuel and food, these were dangerous times for U.S. sailors in the South Pacific.

An analogous incident occurred again, shortly after the war, when an Atlantic Refining P & T Mechanic, without any apparent reference to anything being discussed, suddenly confronted me with, "Bob, I was at Kasserine". Although not well conversant with the U.S. Army's North African Campaign at the time, his tone indicated that it was a touchy subject. He was emotional. And he talked for a long time. Reflecting on that incident, it occurred to me that his reaction was similar to that of the "Boise" sailor... , one of total disbelief! And probably crossed his mind to say, "Where the hell have you been?" Or, "Get your head out of the sand!"

The battle for the Tunisian Kasserine Pass developed in February 1943... , about three months after the initial November American landings in North Africa. And the disaster of that loss threatened to disrupt the entire strategy of Allied plans carefully laid out at Casablanca.

By February 17th.. , German tanks had forced major American and a few French out of important airfields at Feriana and Thelepte. Having retreated across the barren coastal plain between the Eastern and Western mountain ranges, aided by the British and French, the Americans attempted to halt Rommel's tanks at Kasserine in what appeared to be an irresistible German attack.. . If their positions were overrun, the Allies might find it necessary to pull out of Tunisia.

Having launched a two pronged attack, on February 19th, Rommel directed one column to penetrate the American forces at Kasserine. Suffering a set back... , the American Division scattered, and the battle for Kasserine Pass raged back and forth for 4 days. Out of 30,000 troops taking part, the cost to American forces.... , 300 killed... , 3,000 wounded... , 3,000 missing... . The II Corps requested 7,000 replacements. Eisenhower, guarded in his comments on Kasserine.. , was upbeat in his assessment for his green troops, "They (the troops) made steady improvement throughout the fighting... , and turning it around... , it turned the tide in Tunisia." One of those taken prisoner, Lieutenant Colonel John Waters, General George Patton's son-in-law, was not set free from a camp deep inside Germany until the final days of the war.

Ultimately relieving General Lloyd R. Frendenhall with General George Patton, Eisenhower had already sent for Major General Earnest N. Harmon, Commander of the 2nd Armored Division. Not to take over the II Corps or bring his division to the battle, Harman was to take charge of the "battle in progress" at Kasserine. To drive the Germans out of the pass and specifically to "lend his advice and leadership". Eisenhower, ever concerned with taking responsibility, provided Harman typewritten orders placing him in charge of "the battle in progress". And Ike pushed British General Sir Harold Alexander to regroup the American troops.

To push back the Germans, Ike told Alexander, his overall commander, that he would "scrape the bottom of the barrel, rob the Fifth Army, Casablanca and Oran...., even send to the states for more men and supplies." To the chagrin of Eisenhower, Field Marshall Irwin Rommel, fearing that the Allied "build up" had too much additional strength, secretly withdrew his forces. Allied forces pursued the Germans as fast as they could lift the mines or get around heavily mined roads and blown up bridges. Vindicated, by August, the 7th Army had taken 96,000 prisoners and inflicted 10,650 dead and wounded upon the enemy. Many believe that Harmon's part in that battle has never been properly recognized.

As with the Boise Sailor... , and the Atlantic "P and T" mechanic... , it is understandable that their war centered around a narrow personal experience. As over 50 years have passed, and as has long been the case with the Civil War, slowly details continue to dribble out a history of WWII. It seems destined to continue for a long time to come.

Penn had been assigned 12 of a total of 150, already on active duty Coast Guard enlisted men, qualifying for the program. Most seemed to have had their earlier training in nearby New Jersey..., at the Cape May Coast Guard Station. Reporting that July morning in whites, exactly the same as those of their Navy counterparts.. , each man displayed a small blue Coast guard shield on their lower left sleeve. Billeted in E.F. Smith, Company "A", Third Platoon, had at least one of those Coast Guard Sailors. "Hooligan's Navy" discontinued it's participation by January 1944.

Activated also on July 1st, the University's 230 man N.R.O.T.C...., Naval Reserve Officer Training Corps.. , reported in uniform that same morning. With their Midshipman type uniforms, and special curriculum, initially they appeared to have an advantage. Among less visible advantages, the "Rotcy" began by enjoying special priorities in billeting and "chow" lines. When it was established that they were not classified as "commissioned midshipmen", the rules changed those advantages. Qualifying for neither the vantages of wearing "bell bottoms" or officer "dress blues", frequently proved to be somewhat inhibiting... , especially when on "liberty". BuPers had also classified R.O.T.C. personnel as Apprentice Seamen.

Between July 1, 1943 and June 30, 1946, the NROTC accepted only applications from those within the V-12 ranks. When the program was disbanded, those V-12s in the NROTC unit were placed on inactive duty and permitted to complete their degree in a civilian status.

At the end of the second term, with the entire Battalion present in Irvine on February 28, 1944, forty-six NROTCs, appointed Ensigns in the United States Naval Reserve, took the "Oath of Acceptance of Office"... .

With Captain Lemuel M. Stevens, USN (Ret.), presiding over the ceremony, the new Ensigns and the V-12 Battalion were addressed that night by the President of the University, Thomas Sovereign Gates. At the famous Curtis organ that night, Joseph D. Chapline, Jr., and the V-12 Chorus provided the music. The Invocation and Benediction were by Reverend J. Clemens Kolb, Chaplain of the University of Pennsylvania.

Although there would be a sizable exodus in the first weeks, with approximately 500 basic men assigned (other than ROTC), Penn was one of the larger V-12 contingents. Tested early on for scholastic aptitude, psychological profile for war, and the U.S. Naval Officers aptitude profile, earlier they were subjected to a ridged physical exam given at the Naval facility nearest to the individuals home. For me, it was Widener Building, on Chestnut Street in center city Philadelphia, a few yards west of the John Wanamaker Department Store. Although that particular exam necessitated a four hundred mile trip by railroad, the center city facility was the nearest to my parent's home. There was no alternative. I have no trouble remembering the name of the Navy Doctor, Commander Burrows, the father of a grade to high school "Billtown" classmate.

During and subsequent to the war, numerous Navy and Marine Corps officers encountered had also passed their initial physical in the Widener Building. Early testing began a continuous process in all categories, a trainee could never be confident that he was "home free". Penn men became accustomed to seeing friends suddenly disappear for some unknown reason... Usually a condition that had surfaced during the continuous testing. Those routine evaluations by the Navy would continue for the entire time they served on active duty.

Early in March, 1943, a Navy "PR" release, published in newspapers across the country, including The Philadelphia Inquirer, The Philadelphia Bulletin, and The Grit (Williamsport), read ...., "The potential officers.. , who will be trained for the Marine Corps and Coast Guard as well as the Navy..., will be chosen by selection boards composed of one Naval Officer, a representative of the public.., and an educator. ." The Navy made certain that there would be at least one Selection Board in each state.

As could have been expected, there were plenty of lines to stand in that Thursday morning. Allowing the new sailors time to become acquainted, lifetime friendships often began while waiting outside Irvine. And it was frequently the way that roommates were assigned when the line moved forward and a Yeoman "logged in" each man's orders. Reviewing and stamping the date and time on each page of each set of orders, before waving him in the direction of the Quad, the Yeoman marked and recorded the room assignment in his "billeting log". And the sailor next in line often became a roommate for at least the next 4 months.

A room assignment and a copy of the regulations in hand, Penn sailors headed West on Spruce Street looking for "Towers" Dorm Entrance to the Upper Quad. Locating the entrance to "Edgar Fahs Smith" Number 20 required returning to the bottom of the "Junior Balcony" steps. Later we would discover that we had been sitting and standing at Irvine all that morning not far from E.F.S.'s statue where, sitting pensively in front of Weightman Hall for almost a century, he had turned green. Often to be repeated by many through the years right up until the present, for most it was the first time to take that walk up Spruce Street... . A few V-12s, passing it for the first time on that sizzling July day, even had their children born in that wing of the University Hospital bordering Spruce Street.

A very special event occurred there on a warm morning, in September, 1948, when my 8 pound 15 ounce daughter, Cynthia Gail, was born.

Assembled in Irvine the week of the 4th, the V-12s were welcomed and addressed by their Commanding Officer, a distinguished white haired gentleman with tremendous military bearing, and a fatherly personality, Captain Lemuel M. Stevens, U.S.N. Retired. Captain Stevens introduced his Executive Officer... , Lieutenant H. S. Rummel, U.S.N.R., who appeared to fit the stereotype and had the personality of a college professor. And met the two officers, with whom we would regularly be in contact on a daily basis, Lieutenants Newpher and Walsh. Always available for spontaneous advice..., both of these officers were exceptionally well suited to their assignment. If their choice was any indication of the caliber of the Navy's WWII assignment selection process, then it can only be categorized as "top notch".

Ask any Penn V-12, and they will readily recall especially pleasant memories of their friendship with Lieutenant Jim Newpher. And, because of his very shiny bald head, would be affectionately referred to as "Skinhead"... . But never in his presence! But, when he provided guidance in making a "crossroads" decision, Lieutenant Walsh may have most influenced my future. A constant barrage of war reports, making us anxious to get out to where the action was, led to a decision to not wait for a commission. Though having formally requested a transfer to the Marine Corps, continuing to badger me to "stick" with the unit,

Walsh repeatedly went over the records and status reports in his Bodine office. The Chiefs, all Specialist "A", a very special group of advisors, were directly involved with Lieutenant Walsh in non-academic fitness evaluations. Responsible to report on the day to day progress of the trainees.., they observed and paid particular attention to "physical fitness" and "military aptitude". The substance of Walsh's resuming argument was, if successful in completing at Penn and Midshipman School, South Pacific duty would come sooner than if transferred to Marine "boot".

Walsh persisted and, although at 18... when months seem like years.., his advice prevailed. It would be difficult to fully evaluate the difference that may have made over the ensuing years.

Promptly introduced to a "Navy routine"...., an order issued by the Executive Officer read as follows:

	DAILY	SATURDAY	SUNDAY
CALL FIRST SECTION	0515	0510	0515
POST THE WATCH	0540	0540	0540
REVEILLE	0550	0550	——
CALISTHENICS	0605	0605	——
BREAKFAST FORMATION*	0635	0635	——
FIRST MORNING SICK CALL	0720	0720	0720
FORM FOR INSPECTION	0730	0730	——
SECOND SICK CALL	0800	0800	0800
CLASSES	0800	0800	——
DINNER	1205	1205	1205
CLASSES	1300	——	——
ATHLETICS OR RECREATION	1630-1730	——	——
SUPPER	1800	1800	1800
CALL TO ROOMS	2000	——	2000
TAPS	2300	2300	2300
LIBERTY**	1915	——	——
LIBERTY OVER	2200	——	2400

* THE BATTALION TO MARCH TO BREAKFAST IN COMPANIES AND PLATOONS.
**LIBERTY HOURS WHEN GRANTED.

Issued in a Manual, "STANDING ORDERS AND REGULATIONS", restrictions were numerous and detailed. The 34 notebook size pages of the manual was comprised of regulations covering academic, military and personal life. While it is doubtful, under any conditions.. , that such regulations could be imposed today, it was nothing more than most anticipated.

Supply had set up a temporary building, for the storage and issuing of uniforms and supplies in the back of the Big Quad. On July 1st, Navy Storekeepers issued blankets, linens, and mattresses until almost midnight. Slightly older, draftees, and rated, the storekeepers were usually married and living off base. Shortly after checking out quarters and meeting room mates, the trainees converged on the "supply shack" to pick up their bedding issue. Issued Summer whites the following week, the "uniform of the day" was posted at Bodine and on the "Towers" bulletin board.

By the following Tuesday, University Academic advisors were assigned, classes scheduled, and books and supplies issued. By Thursday, some had easily settled into a Navy-Academic routine. Others would need a few days to make the adjustment. Adjustment.. to Penn.. , to a first college experience.. , to the Navy.. , to Philadelphia.. , to the fact that professors led off with massive assignments.. , to the Philadelphia July heat.. , to the poorly fitted uniforms.. , to the combination routine.. and restrictions.. , to exchange mom's home cooking for that of "H and H".. , to missing the girl friend (V-12's and Midshipmen were prohibited from being married). Adjustment wouldn't wait, the pressure of a high powered schedule, both academic and Navy, took care of that.

In addition to the individual academic curriculum, the Navy's agenda included dress reviews and inspections in the lower "Quad" and the parking lot in front of the Palestra. Held almost every Saturday, sometimes on River Field, the Battalion's dress parades were especially impressive when held on Franklin Field.... The parade uniform was "dress whites" or "dress blues" and always with "boots"... , khaki scrubbed to light tan..., almost white. The "old" Navy took pride in their uniforms and "boots"..., and Penn's sailors had no trouble living up to that tradition. When the unit quickly took on the look of a sharp veteran military unit, dress parades were impressive.. . Quickly learning to tailor and press their uniforms, they could shape and square their hats better than any old "salt" out of the South Philadelphia "Yard". And had readily perfected the "non-regulation" trick of "two blocking" their scarfs (Navy ties) as well as any "hash marked" sailor.. The Navy strove for military comportment and Penn sailors gave it to them "in spades".

There were times when the unit would drill as a Battalion, by Companies, or even by Platoons. With "dress parades" in all types of weather, frequently requiring "P" Coats, Penn sailors marched briskly to music supplied by their own Navy Band. And were reviewed on Navy Day, Armistice Day, on a special Memorial Parade to honor the University.. the 50th Anniversary of the General Alumni Society.. , as well as on other special Penn/Navy or national celebrations. At those parades, Dr. Thomas S. Gates, '93 College, '96 Law, President of The University, would often stand along side of Captain Lemuel Stevens, USN, to review the Battalion.

All during that period, Gates' son had been serving as an officer aboard a 3rd Fleet Carrier. Fourteen years later, then having become Secretary of the Navy, Thomas Gates Jr. reacted knowingly when reminded of his father's wartime association with the Navy V-12. To honor certain World War II Navy and Marine Corps Flag Officers... the best... , the Secretary had been the guest speaker at a testimonial dinner held in May 1957 at New York's Waldorf Astoria.

Billed as "Operation Remember", the occasion paid tribute to those ranking Navy and Marine Corps officers primarily responsible for the magnificent victories of WWII. Flag officers like Chester Nimitz, William "Bull" Halsey, Holland "Howling Mad" Schmidt, and Raymond Spruance. Captain Draper Kauffman, Gates's Naval Aide, with whom I had become associated while assigned duty with one of the first U.S. Navy Underwater Demolition Teams (Navy Seals), had assisted in arranging the occasion. It was due to Kauffman's gracious foresight that an invitation arrived in the mail. Recalling parades on Franklin Field, of his father's participation, Gates, a Penn Man, responded with reminiscences of his father's wartime letters detailing experiences with the V-12.

Spontaneous loyalty, readily generated for both Penn and the Navy, spawned strong life long attachments to both by these willingly impressionable young men. The centuries old rich histories of the two institutions inspired the new Penn Navy men to enthusiastically embrace their colorful traditions.

Not as visible as they would have been in a normal peace time circumstance, the two faculty advisors providing advice to me during that period are recalled with great affection. Starting off with an indoctrination in the Wharton School curriculum, Wharton Professors Dr. John Albrecht and Dr. Victor Stanislaus Karabaz provided direction in choosing a course schedule for the initial semester. Also a major change for them, the proposed curriculum necessarily required the inclusion and scheduling of Naval Sciences... , Calculus and Trigonometry, Physics I and II and Engineering Drawing I and II. New to Penn and Wharton, with little concept of what a heavy schedule could be, I followed the advice of advisors who were apparently convinced I was ready to handle 24 credits. Apparently they had been under the impression that it was necessary to follow the Wharton minimum plus the Navy requirements. Shortly thereafter, a congenial young statistics professor provided the counsel to reduce the course load to 21 credits.

It could be generally construed that V-12's were motivated by two different objectives. One group aspired to get the required courses behind them as quickly as possible, achieve a commission by completing Midshipman School, and to be assigned immediately to Sea Duty. And there were those of another "school of thought", maybe less romantic, and they had as their objective to seek the most education for the longest period of time. For those in the latter category, those seeking other than a "Line Officer" commission, BuPers would occasionally assign appropriate college courses.

Those seeking a "Deck" or "Line" Officer Classification would learn their trade at Midshipman School. With it's strictly Naval Sciences curriculum, including courses in Navigation, Naval Ordinance, Seamanship, Communications, Damage Control, Recognition, Ship Handling etc., these men graduated prepared to become "seagoing" professionals.

Including substantial doses of Commander Gene Tunney's rigorous physical training and swimming agenda, the Navy intended to insure, in fact required, individual fitness. In khaki shorts and white "tee" shirts..., sweat suits in colder weather..., the 0600 muster in the "Lower Quad" included the first workout of the day. Conducted by a Chief Petty Officer, visible on a six foot high platform, no matter what the weather, the sailors did twenty fast minutes of non-stop calisthenics. Deep knee bends, squat thrusts, push ups, jumping jacks, body bends, running in place..., and a lot of other early morning agony.

Instituted immediately after July 1st at Penn, the new sailors began their individual conditioning with, "The Navy Standard Physical Fitness Tests". Referred to by the Chiefs as "strength tests", the V-12s were tested separately in six basic categories; 1.) squat thrusts; 2.) sit ups; 3.) 100 yard dash; 4.) pullups; 5.) squat jumps; and 6.) push ups.

Having already caught the beginning of the fitness training trend sweeping the country in high schools and colleges, the sailors were already at ease with most of the "tests". Most could handily do over 150 sit-ups, 40-50 push-ups and 30-35 pullups. The "squats" were new and were timed. And were probably responsible for a few knee problems down the road. However, after about 16 weeks of conditioning, there were a few that could not meet the minimum standards. And they were dropped from the program.

The most motivating factor was the individual competition, more sit ups, more pull ups, faster 100 yards etc. than your roommates.. , a friend.. , the guy doing sit-ups next to you.. , the guy holding your legs.. , etc. .

Lieutenant D.C. Bailey, head of the Athletic Department, kept a card file with individual records. Maintained by the "Chiefs", laggards were called in and warned that it was necessary for them to meet the minimum requirements of the program. And by Autumn, as the sailors became better conditioned, the minimum scores were revised upward.

The obstacle course at River Field was not much of a challenge... Compared with most.. , probably a poor excuse. Instead, the V-12s would run down to "River Field", up and down the stairs next to the Power Plant, over the obstacle course, and then back to Weightman.

Almost any infraction of any of the regulations, or unsatisfactory conduct, would pull a little "happy hour" for Saturday afternoons. With their Saturday afternoons thoroughly employed down on River field, it frequently meant restricted to the base and an early "sack time" on Saturday night. Those who drew that duty would find themselves in a lot better condition on Sunday morning. Since it also required that a Chief had to stick around and work the condemned, the warmhearted spirit was not pervasive. It meant that he had to take his crew for a workout down on steaming hot, or freezing cold, "River Field". In snow, rain, heavy humidity, or lung piercing industrial haze and stench...., the Chief would stand in the center of the grass field and direct this weeks transgressors in a series of workouts. "Duck waddle" for a half hour, half hour of "jumping jacks", fifteen minutes of "push ups", half hour of "double timing" around the perimeter of the field, half hour of squad "close order" drill, half hour of running up and down the stairs next to the power plant, etc. . River Field could always be counted on to be a dismal place on Saturday afternoons. But about halfway through the dreary session, the aching "happy hour" sailors began to ponder a "Horn and Hardart's" Saturday night dinner of baked beans and hot dogs. Famous for it's tasty crocks of deep brown baked beans, the Navy also insisted they be served, in Navy tradition, at breakfast.

Whenever the Delaware Valley weather was exceedingly stormy or rainy, as it occasionally is, calisthenics were sometimes held in Weightman or Hutchinson Gym. In bad weather, also taking advantage of Franklin Field Stadium, running or drilling sessions would be held under the outer covered perimeter. Regardless of the weather, all early morning calisthenics were held in the "big quad".

When strength tests improved very markedly, permitting some fun and competition, football, softball, volleyball and basketball became part of the fitness docket. Judgements were made on individual abilities and applied to the personnel cards in Lieutenant Bailey's file. Acting in the capacity of "scouts", the "Specialist A" Chiefs would assist the coaches by calling attention to those excelling in basketball or football. Shortly thereafter, those men would receive a personal invitation to come out for the team from Football Coach George Munger or Basketball Coach Don Kellett.

Though the Battalion was loaded with athletes, a varsity team sport could not assist in their academic scholarship in any manner.. . Not wanting to risk the time, and jeopardize their chances to move on to Midshipman School, frequently Penn sailor's felt compelled to forego varsity sports.

As a part of the curriculum, there were a few sparsely productive sessions in boxing and wrestling. With big heavy gloves, so big and heavy that it was often ridiculed as boxing with pillows…, it was impossible to do any damage. And with "arms length" instruction, wrestling consisted of a lot of close up grunting, groaning, and grappling with another none too fragrant male. Not very enticing to a young virile sailor with a high level of testosterone!

At Penn, the Navy Chiefs were notoriously not adept in the water; most of the coaching was given "by the book".. , standing at the side of the pool. Penn V-12s rarely ever experienced seeing a Chief in the water! Taking place in both Weightman and Hutchinson pools, swimming tests were thorough.. , but not difficult. And to pass the "First Class" test, simply swim freestyle 220 yards in a reasonable time, swim the length of the pool under water, break a few life saving "holds', demonstrate a few "tows' and demonstrate the use of the "bellbottoms" as a life preserver. A lot of fun, the latter involved flinging a pair of white Navy "bellbottoms" with "tied legs" overhead in such a manner that they would gather air. Once filled with air, they acted as a "life preserver" for a sailor lying between the inflated legs. And it worked!

Having classified the sailors into 1st, 2nd and 3rd class swimmers, training was gradually stepped up. And at Penn, instructors paid particular attention to the obvious predicament of a sailor whose ship had been sunk.

Weightman pool, fitted out with a broad "cargo net" and a couple of "Jacobs' Ladders"…, allowed the fully uniformed sailors to simulate climbing out of the water to board a rescue ship.

For a guy who spent his Summers on the river at the Susquehanna Canoe Club, or on the lake up in the mountains at Eagles Mere, the 1st class test turned out to be a "piece of cake". And, because the swimming season would be over before being age eligible, received his "Life Saving" certification a few months early.

Having been qualified by a volunteer civilian Red Cross Instructor, 38 percent of the Penn Men earned their Red Cross Life Saving Certificate.

A select group of professional and former college athletes, the Navy Chiefs, designated Specialist "A", were eminently qualified to implement Tunney's physical training program. And U of P Chiefs were outstanding! During WWII, specialist ratings, based upon civilian expertise, were sometimes granted prior to entry into the Navy. An "A" in the rating chevron stood for "Athletic".

And those recruited former athlete "specialists" also played a significant additional instruction role during V-12 indoctrination. Advancing former Penn V-12s would discover those fitness ratings, recorded in "Qualification Record Jackets", would follow them throughout their Navy career.

A few of the other popular Penn faculty, names that come easily to mind, were Balderston (Dean of Wharton), Dorizas (Wharton, Geog. III), McClelland (Provost), Beal (Trigonometry and Calculus, Bennett Hall), George MacFarland (Wharton, Accounting) and many others who were greatly admired and affectionately remembered.

One, that easily trips the memory of many others as well, is Mike Dorizas. Best remembered for his legendary "Geog. III" course, his classes were always filled and the lecture hall packed. Though brilliantly presented, in his enthusiasm, Mike's thick Greek accent sometimes got in the way. A proxy, with a suite in the Freshman Dorms, Mike had been a popular Penn, and nationally known, athlete before World War I. A native of Crete, wrestling as the "Mighty Greek", Dorizas was an undefeated heavyweight. Short in stature, weighing in at 215 pounds of all muscle, Mike became Eastern Heavyweight Champion in 1913. With a concentration of wrestling on the East Coast at the time, that was tantamount to being a World Champion. Competing in the Olympic games as a weight lifter, he also made a mark as a finalist in the javelin event. And then continued his winning style in the uncomfortable lecture halls of Wharton's enduring Logan Hall.

As an Assistant Professor of Geography at the university, Dr. Michael M. Dorizas launched a series of Geopolitical lectures at 1600 on Fridays in Houston hall. In one of Mike's presentations, he would become intensely emotional in discussing Germany's plan for world domination. And he invoked the names of British Foreign minister Eden, and the then U.S. Secretary of State, Cordell Hull, with whom he apparently had been personally familiar. And he startled the audience when he mentioned that he was an acquaintance (maybe a friend) with Carl Haushaffer, a reputed close friend and confidant of the Nazi Dictator, Adolf Hitler.

And, to men new to Wharton, Dr. George MacFarland was an understanding friend and mentor. Someone that you felt that you could confide in.. , he could have been your dad. Only a few years later, during early years with The Atlantic Refining Company, and it's successor, The Atlantic Richfield Company, I discovered that he did have a son. And I valued a similar friendship and pleasant business relationship with, "a chip off the old block", George MacFarland Jr... .

Tall and thin, with the carriage and appearance of an Ivy School Dean that he was, although remotely friendly, Candby Balderston always seemed to be accessible as he walked the halls of Logan. Though his office door was always wide open in those V-12 years, he was rarely visible to those passing. Located immediately to the left of the entrance on the first floor of Logan.. , that would change radically when the old hands returned after the war. For some reason, by then, he had arranged his desk so that he could be readily seen through the office door.

And it had often been stated with pride, by upper classmen and professors, that Wharton was strictly for men... , no woman had ever taken a class in Logan Hall! In emphasizing that fact, even the Dean seemed to enjoy a touch of satisfaction.

For those returning to Penn in the Autumn of 1946, reviewing the veteran's accrued assembled records, Dean Balderston took on the special assignment of personally approving their transferred credits; prior college, AAF college training, Midshipman School, special training, A.S.T.P. etc. . And he expressed enormous interest in the details of what had happened to V-12s after leaving Penn. He was particularly insistent in pursuing details concerning the Navy's Midshipman School at the University of Notre Dame. But then spent most of the two hours fixated on details concerning the operations of Underwater Demolition Teams. And wanted to know all about the training and facilities at Fort Pierce and Maui, life aboard ship and in the islands, as well as Japan. In earlier years, Balderston left an impression of being aloof.. , not readily accessible. But by the Fall of '46, his interest, in finding out about those personal intervening war years away from Penn, dominated the interview. And that session has become the lasting hallmark of my recollection of Dean Candby Balderston.

Advanced mathematics courses, having been prescribed by the Navy as a part of the V-12 curriculum, even caused Wharton Men to find it necessary to schedule courses away from Logan Hall, Hare Building, and College Hall. And there was a natural curiosity and testosterone attraction to walk the extra distance for a first time occasion of a class or two in the "Women's College".

Crowding into "funeral parlor quiet" Bennett Hall, the sailors met their kindly frail and elderly Math professor for the first time. At first... , Professor Beale... , accustomed to instructing mostly Penn Women... , seemed almost disconcerted by the bustling invasion of "white hats" to his 2nd floor Bennett classroom. To Beale, they always seemed to be in a rush! Racing in and out of class... , they were always in a hurry to make the next class.. , or the next workout.., or the next drill.. , or library session.. , or study hall.. . Standing in the corridor outside his classroom, Professor

Beale was overheard observing to his friend, Professor Carriss, "I've never heard so much noise in this building... , where the hell did all these sailors come from?"

Never-the-less, there was an spontaneous affinity between the elderly professor and the teenage sailors.

With a pedantic college professor personality, the elderly Beal fulfilled their ideal concept of a "professor". Extremely knowledgeable of his subject.. , he gave the impression that he had no confidence that any of these "always in a hurry" students could ever impress him that they caught on enough to pass his course. It would be difficult to say who was the most surprised when they did.

CHAPTER IV.

"A Memorable Experience"

"Whatever you do next... , in graduate or professional study.. , in business or industry.. , and wherever your lives may lead you.. , I hope that you move on with the satisfaction and the confidence that come rightly to those who have met successfully a real test of achievement. I wish each of you many useful and happy years of happy living."

George McClelland, February 7, 1948

By mid August... , Penn Sailors, not unlike the rest of the military and civilian population, allocated a portion of their monthly pay for the purchase of "war bonds". And by September, 93.4% of the unit subscribed to purchase bonds totaling 21.6%, over one-fifth, of their total Navy payroll.

Cited by the Fourth Naval District, following the official presentation on Thursday October 14, 1943, of the "Commandant's Pennant" for "high achievement in the purchase of war bonds", the Battalion on parade was inspected by Rear Admiral Milo H. Draemal, U.S.N..

The Battalion marched to it's own Navy band, under the direction of C.S. Bush, A.S. U.S.N.R.. And, directed by N.S. Lakis, A.S., USNR, Penn's Navy Chorus lent a choral backup to the agenda with "America" and "Anchors Aweigh". Those in attendance were welcomed by William H. DuBarry, Vice President and Assistant to the President. The invocation was delivered by Reverend J. Clement Kolb, the University Chaplain.

The "Unit Citation" was delivered by Lieutenant Miles Lilly, U.S.N.R., Coordinator of War Bonds, Fourth Naval District. And the "Commandant's Pennant" was presented by Commander Scott G. Lamb, U.S.N., (Ret.), Director of Training, Fourth Naval District.

Accepting the pennant, Captain Lemuel M. Stevens, U.S.N. (Ret.), Commanding Officer, Naval V-12 Unit, University of Pennsylvania, on behalf of the battalion, received the congratulations of Rear Admiral Milo H. Draemal, U.S.N., Commandant of the Fourth Naval District headquartered at the Philadelphia Navy Yard.

With an extremely beautiful day to accentuate the enclosed stadium setting, the colorful "massed" Battalion parade, executed with practiced precision, is remembered as a very special event for Franklin Field. No stands in back of Weightman Gym in those years... , fewer lanes on a much narrower cinder track.. , astro-turf hadn't been invented. Comprising the battalion, all five companies... , uniforms of freshly scrubbed "whites", spotlessly scoured parade "boots", white hats "squared", and black "ties" "two blocked"... , presented a perhaps never to be repeated occurrence on the cool closely mown green grass of incomparable 1895 Franklin Field.

In awarding the "War Bond Pennant", the Fourth Naval District Commander's message read as follows:

Dear Captain Stevens:

Heartiest Congratulations to you and the personnel of the Navy V-12, University of Pennsylvania Unit, for their splendid War Bond participation.

These men are to be commended, not only by reason of qualifying for the V-12 Program, but also of their evidence of demonstrating that a Country worth fighting for is worth investing in.

Kindly extend my congratulations to all hands who have made this possible.

Sincerely,
s / M.H. Draemel
Rear Admiral, U.S. Navy
Commandant

By the end of October, many of those reporting to Penn in July were bound for other assignments. To Naval Air training, to "boot camp", to Midshipman School, to civilian status, returning to the fleet, etc.; the original contingent was conspicuously depleted. In a matter of hours, those departed had been replaced by 300 newly arrived sailors.

One hundred and ten petty officers from other active duty commands, as well as the fleet, presented their orders to the Duty Officer in Bodine. Having been gleaned from a tremendous number of applicants, they had been selected because of their service records as well as their scholastic background. And had received the strong endorsement of their commanding officer.

Along with the 75 reporting from basic aviation training, 40 June high school graduates, coming directly from civilian life, having had their active duty status previously postponed, "logged" in several hours later..

Checking in at the same time, from fifty-five colleges and universities throughout the country, a fourth group of 75, were advanced students in their various fields . With approximately 850 V-12 sailors matriculating that November, more than 300 had advanced to the status of medical or dental students... , or were classified as members of the Naval Reserve Officers Training Corps.

It was immediately apparent to those new to Penn and Phila-delphia that, for over 150 years into the early 1940's, Philadel-phians had a proclivity for the Navy. It was a "Navy Town"... , with all of it's implications. Although located at the "headwaters" of Delaware Bay, and not an "Operating Base", the "Yard" was a busy port providing lots of Navy so as to keep a sizeable Shore Patrol contingent active.

Commissioned in early 1943, the crew of the new 45,000 ton Battleship New Jersey went on completing it's "fitting out" while getting a "hands on" understanding of the ship. With massive Dry Docks, and the reputation for having one of the finest ship repair units in the world, the Philadelphia Yard was frequently the destination for battle damaged ships from all of the Navies of the Free World. You could find British, French, Norwegian, Dutch, Canadian and Polish sailors on liberty in the most remote sec-tions of the city. Encountered following the war, their folks at home would later recall to those visiting from the U.S., that Philadelphians had been great "war time" hosts to their Navy.

With a wide range of relationships somehow infiltrating the West Philadelphia campus, Penn Men did not confine their interest in female companionship to Bennett Hall (Women's College) and Sergeant Hall (Women's Dorm). Probably having a lot to do with the wartime disposition of the civilian population, the sailors were invited to socialize with ladies from every direction in the Delaware Valley.

Persevering in the pursuit of their academic and navy studies, only a few sailors found Philadelphia's reputation as a city of "female pulchritude" to be detrimentally distracting. To the majority, merely a passing benevolence to indulge sparingly on the limited "liberty" time. Avoiding the constant concern of "bilging out", the Penn Sailors deflected the always ominous threat of a transfer to "boot camp" by "cracking the books" and "burning the midnight oil". Both essential to Midshipman School acceptance.

With no shortage of all types of social invitations, Penn Men were welcome in the suburbs as well as in the city. One sailor, having been around horses all of his life, and with excellent equestrian skills, when introduced to "fox hunting" by a Penn friend, discovered Chester County horses to be quite a change from the rugged Western horses that he rode at home. A revela-tion to the Penn coed, she described his riding style as, "something out of the movies".

Often seen walking through the campus, pretty dark haired Irish lasses, living close by on narrow cobblestone streets, were romanced in neighborhood rathskellers and under quaint colonial gaslights. Riding the "El", subway, and trains downtown from North Philadelphia neighborhoods... , as well as Manayunk, Olney, Germantown, and Frankford, blue eyed and blonde, the Polish and German damsels caught a "42" car going West on Walnut to tryst with Penn sailors on their West Philly campus. Convenient to all types of transportation, the popular center city "USO Plaza", opposite the Pennsy's Broad Street Station and City Hall, was a magnet for the entire Delaware Valley. And a place for the Penn Sailors to meet up with comely dark eyed Italian gals from neighboring South Philadelphia.

To find their way around the Delaware Valley, V-12s rode the Reading, the Pennsylvania Suburban line, the "37" car, the Chester 13 trolley, the "El", the subway, and the "Red Arrow Line". One guy even staked his reputation on the Camden Ferry. After leaving Mr. James's Ballroom, or dropping off their date at Bryn Mawr or Harcum, passing through the "69th Street" Terminal in the early hours of morning, they caught an almost empty "El" into the 40th and Market stop.

A popular 69th Street dance emporium, with a rotating mirrored ball on the ceiling, Penn Sailors "tripped the light fantastic", and romanced the gals from West Philadelphia and the Main Line until the "wee" hours, with "Mr. James". Invited coeds, from the numerous Delaware Valley schools, traveled to West Philadelphia to attend V-12 campus dances. And the Penn sailors reciprocated by attending their tea and class dances. Just around the corner at 34th and Spruce, the neighboring U of P Nurses School was restricted almost as much as that of V-12s. Occasionally leading to lifetime relationships, circumstances in common did nothing to discourage campus romances... . And sailors, surprised in the act of meeting their nurse in a clandestine rendezvous in one of the numerous "niches" of the sprawling campus, were soundly ignored by the congenial campus cops.

Foiled, when surprised by her stern interceding pietistic father, one smitten V-12 had made elaborate plans to elope to Elkton, Maryland. Caught when loading their rented 1939 Studebaker on a cold Saturday in January, his eminently willing and comely young German-Irish love, reluctantly returned to her Overbrook home. In order to prevent his ejection from the officer candidate program, they had agreed to keep their nuptials a secret. Though the war didn't stop, when their correspondence appeared to falter, he blamed himself for being too absorbed in his duties out in the Pacific. Running into each other at Stone Harbor after over twenty years, she related for the first time that his "V-Mail" letter's had been cut off by her vigilant father. Thwarted by her parent's venerable concern over their different religious denominations, the luckless romance ultimately culminated in the frustrated young lady's advocated marriage to a neighbor. Finally acceptable to the father, the groom's predominant qualification was that he attended the same Catholic Parish. Another couple of years would slip by before they met again. And once again they resumed their long smoldering... , almost lost friendship... .

In early March, 1944, delivered to his dorm room, each Navy Penn Man received a small envelope addressed personally. The return address on the envelope read:

Dr. Edward M. Twitmeyer
Girard College
Philadelphia 21, Pa.

And the enclosure read:
The Society of the Alumni of the College
University of Pennsylvania
and
"The Union League of Pennsylvania"
Invite
The Men Of The Navy V-12 Unit
University of Pennsylvania
TO ATTEND A SMOKER
in Lincoln Hall at the Union League
Broad and Samson Streets
Friday March 31, 1944 at 8:15 P.M.
Admission by card only

Guests that March 31, 1944 at a "smoker" held by the University Alumni of the College at the Union League, the Penn Sailors appreciated their Friday night away from the campus. And, considering the wartime shortages and restrictions, it had to be quite a generous undertaking by the Union League. About half of the Battalion accepted the Alumni's invitation to enjoy the cigars and the Union League's exceptionally fine buffet. But it was back to the Palestra and a typical Horn and Hardart breakfast the next morning.

The Schuylkill sailors wasted no time in adopting "Smokey Joe's" as their favorite on campus "watering hole". Markedly different from that of Notre Dame and it's Midshipman School, the difference in the two campus settings is most cogently expressed in their "off hours" gathering places. Unlike Penn's popular "on campus", open to the public, "Smokey Joe's", the gathering place out at South Bend was limited to Notre Dame students and faculty.

Opposite the Alpha Chi Rho House, "Smokey Joe's" was conveniently established in the heart of the campus on 36th Street between Locust and Walnut.... . Located a few wobbly steps North of the Christian Association Building at 36th and Locust, and ensconced in a cellar, the popular bar was readily accessible to the Dorms, the surrounding fraternities, and even redoubtable old Logan Hall (Wharton School). Peanuts were provided in abundance to customers dropping by to quench their thirst with a quick draft. Dropped by the beer drinkers, the bar's floor was usually deep in peanut shells. A popular and fun place, a renown landmark for which Penn had become noted, and with it's door usually wide open... Summer or Winter... , it was often the first destination of visiting Ivy Leaguers. The raucous serenading strains of "Anchors Aweigh", as often as "Drink A Highball", coming out of the usually packed "standing room only" rathskeller, could distract a well intending student sailor from a full session at the library.

By contrast, at Notre Dame, the place to congregate on campus was a soda fountain operated by the University. Fittingly called the "Huddle", and located in a quiet treed setting in the shadow of the famous "gold dome", it was also conveniently close to the few Midshipman billeted in Walsh Hall. Only accessible to the Midshipmen for about an hour after the evening meal, that did not deter them from enjoying one of the Huddle's thick and creamy milk shakes made from milk and ice cream supplied by the University's own herd of holsteins and dairy. Since the only time permitted Midshipmen was immediately after evening "chow", it made it necessary to drink a "shake" on a full stomach. As ham, sausage, and bacon, from the college butcher shop, were served almost daily, milk shakes were popularly in demand to compensate for the steady diet of pork supplied by the University's "pig farm". Dinner over.. , the Midshipmen regularly made a dash across campus for the "Huddle".

But even in the city.. , West Philadelphia.. , you could find a fairly decent milk shake at "Sophomore Sol's". Although Sol sold all sorts of odds and ends, he staked his reputation on having one of the best "juke boxes" in Philadelphia. For a nickel you could hear the latest in popular tunes on campus... ,"Paper Doll", "Chattanooga Choo Choo", "I'll Be Seeing You", "Always", Anchor's Aweigh, "Bell Bottom Trousers". Even the Penn Band's rendition of "The Red and Blue" by Harry Westervelt '98.

Stories, of Sol's significantly exaggerated career, as an undergraduate at Penn, were legendary. One of the most implausible credited Sol with being the only Penn man to flunk "Geog. 3".. . Ever! Mike could be counted on to not break with tradition, he wouldn't flunk anyone!.

And one of Sol's earlier capers had developed into a "rite". Recognized, when walking in front of the Penn stands at Franklin

Field in the Fall, the cheer leaders would grab Sol and pass him up into the stands. Before arriving back on the track, the campus merchant had floated on hands up and down the stands for a half an hour. For "Sol", that could have been designedly in lieu of advertising.

In the heart of the campus, the "Venetian" Restaurant, considered an O.K. place to take a coed date, was located on Walnut Street in a "walk up" store front. You could literally sit in the big plate glass window and, keeping one eye on the "one way" traffic, enjoy the four courses of the day's "blue plate". All for the price of a "buck"!

"Horn and Hardart", with two locations on campus... , had restaurants at 34th and Woodland and 40th and Chestnut. Just West of 34th Street, the "H & H" cafeteria, with frontage on both Woodland and Walnut, could be entered from either street. Easily visible across the sloping "green" of College Hall, it was the chief beneficiary of a large loyal contingent of Penn students and faculty. The Chestnut Street restaurant, on the Western edge of the campus, and featuring "waitress service", was frequented by those living in the surrounding neighborhood which then was considered to be very nice. Along with many of their thrifty students, frequently seen partaking of the 35 cent vegetable platter.., a nickel for coffee.. , but no charge for the rolls.., Penn "Profs" were regulars.

With a deserved reputation for special and generous "Deli" sandwiches... , for the hearty appetite, "Cohen and Kelly" was then located in a store front near the "El" on 37th street. The wiry proprietor stood in front of a case of cold cuts, cheeses, pickles, dressing etc. while the customer just kept on pointing out their choices until the owner said 'nuff.. . Slapping on the top piece of bread,- and cutting it down the middle, the deli man placed it on top of the glass case for the salivating customer.

The "blue plate", for about 50 cents, included generous portions of meat and mashed potatoes smothered with lots of thick brown gravy. Milk and Beer were the beverages. And the popular, if not the only, quantity for both was a quart. Since the honor system prevailed, the restaurant never used checks; on the way out the door you simply told the cashier (also the owner) what you had..., and he would produce a number out of his head. Strictly a "stag" place, it didn't require a eye-catching sign to recognize that the clientele was limited to males.

With a much diminished wartime economy, and the government's admonishment to conserve on everything, men's clothing stores on campus were not thriving. But that did not seem to deter the proprietor of Butz's haberdashery. If Jesse Butz's store wasn't busy, he sure made every attempt to make it look bustling. With or without customers, he could usually be found buzzing around the crowded (with merchandise) aisles of his store... Always piled high with newly delivered merchandise, it seemed to be displayed wherever the delivery man dropped it. An impeccable dresser himself, Butz had a reputation for having a large and attractive inventory, of collegiate style clothing, which only he could find, among the large disorganized display. When the decline of civilian students took it's toll, Butz did his best to replace his loss with business people. Though civilian clothes were scarce, especially white shirts, Butz always had ample of the "hard to find" for his customers. Accommodating to the service people, he did a pretty good business in tailoring on both officer and enlisted uniforms. And, using one of his windows throughout the war to display Navy attire, resulted in the sale of a few uniforms... .

The crafty "Sox Miller", then on Spruce Street opposite 37th Street Towers Dorm entrance, rather than depending on the much depleted civilian student body, had aggressively managed to sustain his business by developing a regular Alumni "off campus" clientele. Walking across the frequently trolley obstructed intersection of Woodland and Spruce, the "bell bottom" sailors would occasionally press their noses to "Sox's" attractively decorated windows to nostalgically "gander" at the display of the latest in "civies". Nonetheless, a V-12s consuming enthusiasm continued to be to gain eligibility to wear the Navy's "blue and gold". "Sox's" large inventory of classic clothes, and appealing windows, would pay off in only a few years when the... , "We Got Back A Little Late... , Pennsylvania '48"... crowd, having shed their uniforms and returned to classes, again became great "Sox Miller" advocates.

Not as in a normal peace time routine, the end of a semester did not mean the usual vacation at home away from classes. With a three semester accelerated year, for those remaining at Penn, the next semester began almost immediately. But the focus of interest for U of P Sailors was the individual orders coming out of Washington.. , from BuPers (U.S. Navy Bureau of Personnel). Having made the grade, and permitted to continue the pursuit of a commission, usually meant reporting within a matter of hours to the campus of one of the three mentioned Midshipman Schools. Those leaving the officer candidate program were frequently issued orders to "Boot Camp" at Bainbridge, Maryland.

Wherever and whatever the duty assignment that followed, many would return to Penn after the war to complete their college courses and obtain a degree. Others returned to the schools where they had initiated their college career... , some would chose another college... , a few opted to make the Navy a career... . And others would altogether reject returning to any college.

After "Hiroshima" and "Nagasaki" jolted the Japs into accepting their inevitable fate, to come to terms on the deck of the Battleship U.S.S. Missouri on September 2, 1945, it gave an all new perspective to the then "off hand", and up till then, optimistic prediction... , "Golden Gate in '48".

The focus having narrowed, before August, Pacific sailors had been totally concentrating on their immediate future. Weeks away, that future had been, "Operation Olympic". And following the Kyushu operation, in the Spring, the invasion of Honshu. Scheduled with the end of the Pacific's typhoon season as a major consideration, a primary concern of the Navy had also been the approaching cold weather and water temperature. Heavy black wool underwear and cold weather alpaca lined "foul weather gear" had already been issued to many in the growing "Olympic" force. Now only weeks away.., "D" Day would quickly be finalized for late October or early November, just about the time that the snow would begin to fly and the water would become intolerably cold. And after that, Honshu was tentatively set for March 1946.

With the abrupt and timely cancellation of those two final operations against the Japanese Islands, as with a hoard of other Navy men, Penn sailors were unexpectedly faced with the need to make a rapid revision in their personal agenda. And trade "Olympic" for a return to the hazards of... , 37th and Spruce... , the reputed "busiest trolley intersection in the world.... And once again Uncle Sam, and The Navy Department, proved to be capable of performing the seemingly impossible. In a remarkable operation, those requesting it were returned to the states and civilian status within a few short months after the September 2nd surrender.

Provost Dr. George McClelland, when welcoming the new Penn men on that hot day in July 1943, had concluded his remarks with the following words first spoken by the University's founder... , and deemed to be significant over two centuries ago:

> *"The idea of what is true merit should also be often presented to youth, explained and impressed on their minds as consisting in an inclination joined with an ability to serve mankind, one's country, friends, and family; which ability is, with the blessing of God, to be acquired or greatly increased by true learning; and should indeed be the great end and aim of all true living".*

> ....*Benjamin Franklin*

While only a few years had passed, a lot of history had been made. And in that intervening time, Dr. McClelland had replaced Dr. Thomas Gates as President of the University. In his new capacity, McClelland would preside over their graduation, hand diplomas to many of those same returning Navy Penn Men, and congratulate the Class of "48". In his remarks to this older group of graduates, President McClelland said:

"Whatever you do next... , in graduate or professional study.. , in business or industry.. , and wherever your lives may lead you.. , I hope that you move on with the satisfaction and the confidence that come rightly to those who have met successfully a real test of achievement. I wish each of you many useful and happy years of happy living."

It was just five years earlier... , that then Provost George McClelland had concluded his welcoming address, on that hot and humid July 1943 day, by wishing those "Navy V-12s".... , *"A Memorable Experience at Pennsylvania"*.

Without exception, it is certain that any returning "Quaker Sailor", many having graduated with the Class of '48... , will agree that it will always be foremost among an exceptional lifetime of memorable experiences.

CHAPTER V.

"Red Faces in Navy Whites"

"With that packed hall coherently unified and totally reverent, and as those of all faiths and denominations prayed together, a young Navy Lieutenant.. , a Chaplain from "the yard".. , led the hushed audience in the Lord's Prayer-. Because they had learned that prayer long before beginning school, it was a rare person that could not recite it under any conditions. No one thought to question the right to pray together in public, a right that our forefathers thought that they had guaranteed and, for which the country, at that very moment, was expending it's youth and it's treasure to preserve."

Enhancing the subdued beauty of the green-gray stone of formidable old Logan Hall, cast by the setting sun, the fading early evening shadows of late Spring barely touched the corner of the gray slate roof of the similarly aging Hare Building, Logan's matching neighbor to the South. And seated vigilantly in his chair in front of College Hall overlooking the campus "green".. , seemingly since it's 1740 inception, old Ben Franklin continued to preside over the University that he founded.

The streets were empty, with no one to listen to them shouting the day's headlines, the "news boys" at the stand on the corner of 37th and Spruce sat around quietly waiting for the delivery of one of the early evening editions of the next days Inquirer or Philadelphia Bulletin.

Except for the trolleys, with their intermittent abrupt noises and vibrations whenever they clamorously switched tracks, followed by clanging bells and trailing periods of a sort of bellicose calm, the Penn Campus was surprisingly quiet... , almost tranquil! And the late Spring freshness, recently accentuated by nature's bright new foliage, filling the voids left by Winter, softened the dormant drabness of the West Philadelphia Campus. It was Spring... , 1944.

Anticipating "orders", many of the Navy men at Penn were looking forward to "shipping out" in a few days to new assignments. With an air of excitement throughout the Delaware Valley, the "City of Brotherly Love" had been anticipating the much publicized USO show and War Bond rally to be held that evening in their Civic Center Auditorium. One of the great auditoriums of the period, both the Republican and Democrat Presidential Conventions had held their debates and endorsed the nominee of their party at the podium of the huge structure.

53

In a relaxed mood, having just shed our "blues" for freshly laundered Summer "whites", Ham and I started out from Edgar Fahs Smith Suite 20 with an acknowledged skepticism that we would be able to obtain tickets to see the show.

An unseasonably warm early May Philadelphia evening with low humidity, the air was clear of the occasional oppressive industrial odors that drifted up from the big war essential factories and refineries of South and Southwest Philadelphia.

An impressive facility for that era, the Civic Center auditorium is located immediately across from the edge of the University's campus, opposite the University Hospital and the then "PGH".., Philadelphia General Hospital.. . The rally would certainly attract war bond supporters from the city as well as all of it's surrounding suburbs for miles in every direction... , including South Jersey. Pennsylvanians were always out in front in their generous and dedicated support of the war effort; this would prove to be one of the most successful and memorable of those events. Not only did Commonwealth citizens give generously from the "family treasury", their sons and daughters volunteered in disproportionate numbers for the services. And the Keystone State's diversified industry provided more than it's share of the arsenal of the free world and the Allied Forces.

With orders already "cut" to report to the Navy's Midshipman School at South Bend, Indiana, at the end of the month, the academic "die had been cast" permitting an "I can spare the time" mood. Our first weekday "liberty" in a many months, and not due to report to a Midshipman School for still another four months, "Ham" could also afford to ease off a bit. Invigorated by the freshness of the weather, relaxed in an unusual for the times "care free" mood, the timing was right to look forward to an evening of light entertainment. That is, it could be.. , if there was a way found to somehow successfully "crash the gate" at the Civic Center.

Though upper Spruce Street was deserted, about the time we passed the University Hospital (*where 5 years later my daughter Cynthia was to be born*), we agreed an exceptionally large number of people were heading in the direction of the "center". Turning the corner at Thirty-Fourth Street, it was obviously a large turnout for a wartime event. On most Spring and Summer evenings during those years, the streets, around the campus and that area of West Philadelphia, were almost deserted. Moving into Thirty-Fourth Street, along with only a handful of men in uniform, we were caught up in a tide of mostly civilians rushing in the direction of the auditorium.

Convinced it would be a full house by the time we passed the "School of Nursing", we resigned ourselves to the fact that obtaining tickets was probably a loosing cause.., doubtful. Starting out, we had visions that somehow tickets would suddenly appear. Our subliminal speculation, probably expecting many "no shows", anticipated a half empty Convention Center. Not appreciated by high priced Hollywood stars.., or encouraging for future bond drives. It was the beautiful weather that made the difference! Anyway, there were plenty of other places, within a short trolley ride, to spend "liberty".

Most attending would have received their tickets by buying, or pledging to buy, a minimum amount of War Bonds. Directly involving the civilian population in the support of the war effort, the highly successful drives to finance it went on without letup. An attempt to keep up with the high cost of supplying the U.S. Forces as well as U.S. Allies made the success of these drives essential. Avidly supported by the public, they would alleviate the conscience of the most dedicated conservative. After the long 1930's "Great Depression", the civilian population was employed at a new high level. And across the country, the little towns were experiencing a little more prosperity, some for the first time. And saving through the purchase of war bonds, allowed them the luxury of putting some savings aside... .

Civilians, even G.I.s, in anticipation of their post war plans and the "good life", were saving in record amounts. And looked forward to a future that the "Depression" and "war generation" folks had never experienced. Though the Navy reported that 93.4 per cent of the Penn V-12s subscribed 21.6 percent of their total payroll for War Bonds, it would not qualify for tickets to the show. It was necessary to make a pledge outside the regular payroll deduction.

Unquestionably the noisily enthusiastic crowd was made up of patriotic Pennsylvanians determined to do their part. Though it was a warm Summer evening, typical of the times, the well dressed crowd wore suits and neck ties. A typical almost entirely white audience of that era, they had no problem outwardly expressing their enthusiasm and support of the war. And contrary to subsequent trends, this crowd was eager to support it with their hard earned cash. Though the "rally" included entertainment, the primary interest of this 1940's crowd was to show their unified support for the country and the war effort. As reported in the late evening edition, "they came `fired up' to openly express their support for a great President, for the armed forces and for the massive civilian effort". The performance of those who worked to supply and arm the forces of all of the Allies had given new meaning to the expression "working around the clock".

Almost to the entrance... , with an army of ticket holders

backed up into long lines, but no tickets available, Ham was told that they expected some to be turned in. Only a short time earlier, our only intent had been to quickly check it out before heading into town. Now our enthusiasm was rekindled by passing conversations with the lightly spirited civilian crowd. Their contagious enthusiasm undoubtedly stoked a determination to find a way to get in.

Not appreciating the extent to which celebrities go to avoid the public, we speculated that we could at least stand outside to glimpse them making their entrance. And, as had happened over and over again in that wartime climate, of lonely strangers among crowds, a sailor on liberty might just undergo the pleasant occurrence of meeting an attractive Philadelphia "gal" with an extra ticket. Not a conscious consideration, a Penn Sailor would not rule it out.

Following the crowd up to the entrance, before we could consider our next move, a "snappily" attired gentleman in a light seersucker suit, and a "USO" tag, confronted us with the hoped for question... , an offer... . With the confidence of someone already knowing the answer to his question, half turning... , looking over his shoulder.. , he asked it anyway, "how would you Navy guys like a front row seat?"

Not even exchanging a glance, Ham gave the gentleman one of his fastest unrecorded affirmatives.

Keeping up his one way conversation, the very amiable official steered us past the crowd, past turnstile lines, and through the main entrance of Convention Center. Keeping our new mentor in sight through the crowded entrance lobbies, we followed him into the cavernous hall which, even at that point, appeared to be almost filled to capacity. Expecting to be left to our own resources once inside, we continued to be surprised when our newly discovered friend propelled us down to the front of the auditorium. Pointing to a pair of empty seats.. , just as he had suggested... , they were "front row".. ! Right at the foot of the raised stage?

Thanking our departing friend, inwardly we could hardly believe our sudden change of luck. And exchanged mutually understanding glances knowing that we would get a lot of "over a beer" mileage from this incident. And for the last half century, it's had it's own place among our repertoire of favorite stories. Without losing any of it's enthusiasm in "the telling", a story that has seen the price of a beer go from a nickel a glass, to as much as four or five dollars a bottle. Yet, that part of the evening became incidental to what lay ahead.

Settling into our temporary folding seats.. , our eyes struggling to adjust to the dark, we could barely make out that the surrounding young men were of similar age and in uniform. Not all were seated in folding chairs.. , some appeared to be in wheelchairs.

Though our eyes were not yet adjusted to the darkness around us... , we could see the distant crowd, in the lighted areas, as they rapidly took seats at all the levels of the noisy and packed Convention Center.

Abruptly.. , without fanfare.. , the lights dimmed... , the noise of the crowd was quickly hushed... , as the band led into a short snappy five minute medley of martial music. With stragglers looking for and settling into their seats, the orchestra took another five minute break before picking up their instruments to begin again with a preamble of flourishes to the national anthem. As if on command, the entire auditorium rose to their feet in unison... .

When the orchestra's beginning efforts were rapidly raised to a recognizable crescendo, the floor beneath the folding chairs began to rumble and shake. In a kind of awkward "side ways" position to the main body of the auditorium, the temporary seats seemed to be moving, no one was certain! With the floor vibrating and shaking, not attempting to stand, Ham and I "stayed put"! To our astonishment... , the floor, folding chairs and all, including those seated, was actually uncertainly beginning to rise just as the orchestra struck up "The Star Spangled Banner". Squinting through the dark across glaring lights, the wide eyed smirk on Ham's face, and the dismay on that of others, became momentarily frozen in place as the floor gradually shuddered and shook it's way up to the same level as that of the stage. With little reason to change expressions, even if they could, those in the temporary seats remained frozen in place as the slow unsteady floor beneath leveled off, stuttered to a stop, and became a part of the stage. All the while the floor level was being raised, controlled from the far reaches of the upper levels, huge flood lights swept back and forth directly across those in uniform. With the final fading notes of the national anthem, remaining on their feet, the audience continued their applause while spotlights played back and forth across the flabbergasted sailors and soldiers.

Under bright spotlights at the center of the stage, standing straight out in response to a stiff breeze manufactured by two large strategically located fans, a huge American flag with it's stirring brightness and color, as only the "Stars and Stripes" is capable, lit up the massive darkened interior of that expansive hall. Other similarly well directed lights, shining down from far up in the "stratosphere" of the auditorium, panned the stage and whipping flag, adding emotional fire to this stirring wartime event. Circling the high upper rim of the darkened remote corners of the building, other fan whipped flags were also "spotlighted" to lend a spirited illumination to the patriotic passion and heightened noise of the charged up crowd throughout the huge center. Well orchestrated, masterfully blending the huge facility to the music and to the audience, the opening for this wartime rally propitiously aroused their patriotic instincts to a deafening pitch.

Contrary to those often voiced, now in vogue, complaints, at that time "The Star Spangled Banner" wasn't that difficult to sing! And the words came easily. The notes weren't too high or too low... no one felt the need to sing it "Blues" style... "Rock and Roll"... "Mo-town"... or "Country". It was just right.. ! Just as old Francis Scott Key had written it.., in 1814, that night aboard ship in Baltimore Harbor.

No one took exception to the fact that it had been written in the shell fire light of battle, nor were they too modest to acknowledge their country was "the home of the free and the brave".

Singing with unabashed "gusto", the audience appeared to be attempting to drown each other out as they strained their collective "apazodiacs" to reach the high notes. Having learned the words to the "pledge of allegiance" to the flag at a very early age, they followed that by singing that old Francis Scott Key anthem at school and at gatherings nearly every day of their lives.

With that packed hall coherently unified and totally reverent, and as those of all faiths and denominations prayed together, a young Navy Lieutenant... , a Chaplain from "the yard".. , led the hushed audience in the Lord's Prayer... Because they had learned that prayer.. , long before beginning school, it was a rare person that could not recite it under any conditions. No one thought to question the right to pray together in public, a right that our forefathers thought that they had guaranteed! And, for which the country, at that very moment, was expending it's youth and it's treasure to preserve.

And as the prayer concluded, and the loud whistles and rustle of those settling into their seats subsided, the crowd sat back prepared to relax and watch the show with it's impressive cast. Less than an hour earlier, Ham and I walked out of "Edgar Fahs Smith" with dubious prospects for ever getting into the rally; perhaps a seat high up near the roof of the cavernous hall.

Following with still another medley of current and patriotic war tunes, this time the musicians put all their emphasis on the hymns and anthems of the armed forces. With most everyone familiar with the words of each during that period, each new rendering brought out enthusiastic audience vocal participation... ; prolonged clapping, whistles and cheers. Singing out the loudest for their favorite, "Anchor's Aweigh" was clearly the obvious winner of the folks in this old Navy port at the headwaters of the Delaware Bay... . Everyone seemed to know the words. As early as 1801, the Philadelphia Navy Yard, having become a bastion of colonial seapower, began building and repairing wooden frigates with the readily available timbers floated down flooding streams from deep in Penn's Woods. And over the next century and a half, William Penn's Quaker city had become well steeped in Navy tradition.

As the musicians finished the opening series, the noisy appreciation of the crowd gradually faded when the lights narrowed to spotlight the "master of ceremonies". Sharply attired in a wool pre-war "tux", rarely seen during those dark times, the "MC" could be seen sweating profusely under the lights. Having waited unnoticed in the shadows near the seated servicemen, gradually he had edged his way over until he stood in the spotlight at the center of the stage.

Enthusiastically thanking the audience for their attendance, support of the war effort, and participation in the bond drive, he then promptly set about to spell out the evening's program. But first he urged the crowd to give a sincere welcome to some very special guests... , "our wounded heroes of our Armed Forces". Turning quickly, he pointed to the group of servicemen to his left... , and then to his right., and announced that these men were recovering veterans from the Valley Forge Hospital and the Navy Hospital at the "Yard" in South Philadelphia. And related that these men had just recently returned from the E.T.O., and the A.T.O., from the desert "front" in North Africa, from the jungle battles of the South Pacific, from the historical Naval engagements at Coral Sea, from destroying four Jap carriers and stopping the invasion forces at the "Battle of Midway", and the defeat of the Nazi's in the "Battle of the Atlantic".

Whenever he paused... for even a moment, or left any kind of an opening... , the audience stamped their feet and continued to burst intermittently into greater applause.

When all other lights were finally darkened, and other spotlights continued to pan back and forth over the uniformed men on stage, the band again swung into an abbreviated medley of the service anthems. In a roar of enthusiasm, when once again the crowd rose to it's feet, this time it took more than five minutes while the Master of Ceremonies waited patiently near the side to finally break in and begin his introduction of the waiting entertainers.

Reconsidering our good fortune, we knew exactly why we had been led to these "super" front row seats in the first place! Seats that had now become a part of the stage! The very accommodating gentleman with the USO needed "bodies".., bodies in uniforms.., sailors to fill space that had been intended for the wounded patients from the two hospitals.

Decidedly uncomfortable, with cheeks "burning red" in the

dark, we had to acknowledge that we had been beguiled by good intentions. And, on the other hand, recognized we would have fun with this occasion as the passing years softened the seriousness of the times.

By then, as the spotlight returned again to the "MC", he moved rapidly in order to take that opportunity to finally introduce the waiting entertainers. With the lights finally moved, the "Red Faces in Navy Whites" were happy to again be hidden and lost in the shadows off to the side of the stage.

Out of the glare of the lights and no longer distracted by the unwanted attention, Ham and I exchanged glances knowing that the "beer mileage" from this foray could be substantially more that we had read into it earlier.

An impressively produced hour of professional entertainment brought repeated appreciative response from the enthusiastic Delaware Valley audience. As many years have passed since that Spring event, the names of most in that group of patriotic entertainers have long since been forgotten. But two of those that I do recall became movie legends... and, a half century later, will be remembered by many. A very young "Oscar" winning actor by the name of Bill Holden and a veteran "song and dance" man, forever remembered for his role in "The Wizard of Oz", by the name of Ray Bolger.

Most noticed by the amused servicemen.., of all the services..., Private Holden was conspicuously uniformed in "tailor made" and well pressed officer "pinks". That would have appeared to have made him "out of uniform"... In Navy parlance.., a violation of Navy "Regs"!

As was regularly the case during that period of uncommon patriotism, the evening's performance wound up with the entire audience rising to sing Irving Berlin's "God Bless America". And suddenly it was over..., the show and rally came to an abrupt end.

Wasting no time, the crowd edged their way out to the street through a wall of opened doors at the rear of the auditorium. Permitting the "going home" audience a feeling of being unified, warm and confident, the band stirred them again as it began to steadily play still another medley of great World War Two tunes..., "I'll Be Seeing You", "The White Cliffs of Dover", "Over There", "Coming in on a Wing and a Prayer", "Remember Pearl Harbor", "I Left My Heart at the Stage Door Canteen"..., and once again , "The Marine Hymn", "Anchors Aweigh", "The Army Airforce Song" and "The Caissons Go Rolling Along".

Exiting into a crowded street, my watch showed that it was precariously near 2100..., reminding me that "liberty" was about to expire. Ham and I would have to hustle in order to arrive back in time to "log in" with the O.O.D. located on the first deck of

"Bodine". A few "open field" maneuvers got us past the "wall to wall" crowd, and out on to Thirty- Fourth, where it began to look as though "logging in" on time would also require a share of luck. Overflowing the street, and crowding the sidewalks, the relaxed "rally" crowd weren't in a big hurry to move very fast in any direction. And not in any big rush, gathered in groups, blocked traffic, and made it difficult for a couple of sailors in a hurry. With "coupon" gas rationing, and an abundance of convenient "PTC" public transportation, very few had chosen to drive their aging family auto. Taking advantage of a pleasant Spring evening, the crowd took it's time sauntering uncertainly in the direction of the trolley and subway stops on Woodland Avenue and Market Street.

Rounding the corner of Spruce and Thirty-Fourth, along side the Hospital and across from Irvine, we broke into a "jog" just about the time a siren abruptly let go with a blast from behind us. Reacting as if on a command handed down from on high to Moses, the crowd parted to make way for a police car which was followed second in line by an open white Cadillac convertible with Bill Holden and Ray Bolger sitting high up at trunk level on the back of the rear seats. Seated at their feet, two grinning Penn sailors. Slowing down momentarily to hold up the procession, the white convertible pulled over to the curb just long enough for Holden to call out, "Hey sailor... , how `bout a lift"? With less than two short blocks to the Tower's entrance, thanking him, we declined. Still "on the double" when passing through the Tower's exceptional curvilinear entrance, the "triangle" in front of "Bodine" was deserted. And.. , the hour being late, two sailors were overdue to "log in" and, to get back to their quarters in Smith.

With the room deserted and quiet at the "Officer of the Deck's" post in Bodine, it made it a little less intimidating to discover the individual standing watch was our old friend, and occasional mentor, Lieutenant James "Skin Head" Newpher. Appreciative of all of the concern he had extended from the earliest days, and warmly recalled for his shiny bald head, Newpher could always find a way to provide a little supporting encouragement. And that night would be no exception. Knowing the Lieutenant would appreciate a brief recounting of our "liberty", afterward he cautioned that we were running close and better hustle on over to E.F. Smith.

Arriving back on the deserted quiet second deck of "Smith", there was an hour left before "tattoo" would be sounded by the bugler posted at the top of the stairs on "Junior Balcony"... , right outside the windows of E.F.S. Number 20.

And with "lights out" in force at 2200, Ham and I had a short hour to compare notes, recall details and file them away for future nostalgic debates over a beer or two at some cool dark dungeonous tap room on a warm Spring evening. All the ironic particulars of a couple of "red faces in Navy whites"... , a couple of sailors in a crowd on that balmy night down by the Schuylkill.

Of course it was an experience that Fred "the Mop" Halkett, our friend and room mate, whether he wanted to or not, would be required to endure before seeking the solitude of his upper bunk.

CHAPTER VI.

"A P-47 Pilot Pitches a Little Navy Liberty"

"The Army assigned a group of eminent psychiatrists to determine the best way to select soldiers for duty on the various fighting fronts. After many tests the learned professors made their report. The best way to find out whether a soldier would be more effective in the desert or in the North was to ask him, "What kind of weather do you like..., hot or cold?" .... Source Unknown

Returning from evening chow, a note pinned to the door of E.F. Smith 20 said simply, "See the OOD for a message from Lieutenant Bob Allen. 2nd Lieutenant Robert Lee Allen, USAAF, apparently had quite a lengthy conversation with the yeoman on duty... Having passed along a New Jersey phone number, Allen's message also stated the hours when he would be available for a return call. And the yeoman also seemed to know the details of Allen's story. My classmate, from 1st grade through high school graduation, was being shipped out. Uncertain as to when, he expected to be in the states only a day or two longer.

Picking up a bunch of nickels, dimes, and quarters at the Quad shop, later when I returned his call, the operator was able to connect with his base orderly room. Managing to have him paged, after a short wait, interspersed with dropping in additional coins when the three minutes were up, he finally came on the line. His P-47 Fighter Squadron was being held over in New Jersey..., at Fort Dix..., not far from Philadelphia. Uttering something about strafing the wrong target..., being rushed out of the country.., leaving the details to be filled in, I guessed that he was in a "staging area" waiting to be shipped out.

Expecting me to somehow get a pass and join him in pitching a last stateside liberty, he could still make it over to Philly that night. Not the best brightest idea he had ever had..., I told him to come on over the next evening and I would do my best to get liberty. As soon as we hung up..., I knew that to have been a foolish assumption. There would be no liberty granted for that purpose.

Arriving shortly after chow the next evening, we met on the street at Towers entrance and, with lots of activity at that hour, slipped into E. F. Smith. Until after the "house captain" stuck his head in the door for the usual study check, I kept him in and out of the closet for about an hour.

Although it usually came down to which Chief had the watch, a "bed check" was to be regularly conducted by the Chief with the "duty". Now if it was Chief Garber or "Big Jack" Stevens, you could forget about it. They would never go through the dorms climbing all those stairs. But if the "Duty Chief" was Hanken or Serfoss..., if they didn't see your head sticking out, they'd pull back the covers to take a look.

Couldn't wait that long to see who had the duty.., it was Allen's last night and he was impatient to get out of there. Managing to set aside images of writing my mother and father to explain all this from "boot camp' at Bainbridge, shaping it in the form of a body, I stuffed a pillow or something bulky in the lower bunk. Anyway, my mother, having known Bobby Allen and his family since he was a little boy, would continue to believe he could do no wrong.

Pulling on my dress jumper, we turned off the lights and made our way unseen to the first floor dorm entrance. Pausing for just a few seconds with the door slightly ajar, as far as we could observe, the "coast was clear" in the Quad. Pushing a little further out to the walkway, it appeared to be totally clear of any personnel.. , civilian or Navy.. . Eyes straight ahead..., we started to walk briskly across the Quad, hoping to pause in the sanctuary of Hamilton Walk, before climbing the back fence. A beautifully landscaped promenade, bordered by majestic old trees that even then seemed to be out of place in this urban University setting, Hamilton Walk was a shaded retreat from the campus's busy city streets. Running parallel to the rear of the South row of old brick dormitories of the "Quad" and the "Triangle", it was bordered by the Philadelphia General Hospital on the East and the Medical Laboratories, MacFarland Hall, the "green house", and the Zoological Laboratory on the West.

Passing the half way point in the center of the Quad's diagonal flagstone walkway, coming from somewhere up on Junior Balcony, we were startled out of our growing confidence by a very clear, "halt and identify yourself"!

For a V-12, that was tantamount to identifying yourself for a quick ticket to Bainbridge "Boot Camp" early the following morning. And a prompt end to any idea one might have had concerning obtaining a commission in this man's Navy. Later, when I took the time to examine the events of that evening, I wondered if Allen has ever considered what a good friend he had that night.

Having already contemplated the potentials should an "hostile" sentry appear, and the tentative mitigation, my response was a stammered, "let's go". And with those whispered words, we both broke into a run and headed straight toward the cover of Hamilton Walk. Having discussed it ahead of time, Allen was aware that all that really separated us from a shot at "liberty", before finding cover within the grounds of either the University or Philadelphia General Hospital, was a six foot wrought iron fence with pointed spikes along the top. In "19 year old" obstacle course style, the fence was scaled in a matter of seconds.

Uniforms intact, we dropped unscathed to the concrete walk leading to the rear entrance of "PGH". Breathing a bit easier, a fleeting concern that we might have been trapped was dispelled when, the only apparent door out of there, the lighted entrance to the hospital was unlocked. Relying on the same "sixth sense" that triggered a spontaneous reaction to the sentry's directions, when confronted by nurses, we made an attempt to act as if we belonged.

Not taking the time to respond to the startled reaction of the hospital personnel, we hurried to find a way out through the front entrance into the cool night air on Curie Avenue.. Curie was then an extension of 34th Street.

From there it was only a short walk to the "El" on Market Street, or to one of numerous trolleys constantly passing the intersection of Woodland Avenue and Walnut Street. Almost any car would take us someplace downtown. And, at that time, anyone in a service uniform could ride the PTC free. Grabbing a "42" car.., a Chestnut Street trolley.. , we headed toward center city. Downtown we knew that we would be inconspicuous among the many servicemen that converged on Philadelphia from the many bases and staging centers from miles around the Delaware Valley.

Open to anyone, not just service people, the old time "free lunch" at the "Budweiser Bar" furnished a lot of lure for downtown Philadelphians. And not only because of the modest tab. Along with tankards of draft beer, the food was almost always fresh and tasty. Located on 15th Street just South of "Broad Street" Station and Market Street, we got off the "42" car at 16th.

With big frosted mugs of cold draft beer, the bountiful buffet had..., all the good stuff that goes with a good lager.. , sharp cheeses, German baloney, Braunschweiger, baked hams, Limburger, pumpernickel, German Dills, Pickled eggs, hot mustard, Pimento cheese, Pickled Herring...., even some rock hard pretzels. Strictly a "stag" saloon, the company owned "Budweiser Bar" was operated by the prominent St. Louis brewer. And Penn sailors were connoisseurs enough to appreciate the traditional ambience, the lunch, the measure of the dime beers, and the generous Busch hospitality.

Knowing full well that it was usually crammed with some of Philadelphia's prettiest brunettes.., frequently from South Philly

Italian families, we started down Locust Street for McGettigan's bar.

East of Broad we passed a few Marines.., six to be exact.., most likely on liberty from the Navy Yard, and seeking to open another war front. "Gyrenes" are noted for wrapping their "Sam Brown" belts around their hands when looking for a fight. And the Marines already had theirs off! Having just passed two Shore Patrol without being checked for "passes", our maneuver was less audacious..., but an old one! Slipping down a narrow gas lighted alley..., we got the hell out of there!

After a few beers, a lot of singing, and a little dancing with the neighborhood friendly McGettigan crowd..., and otherwise an uneventful evening..., Allen caught the last bus across the Ben Franklin Bridge to New Jersey. Serving out the rest of the war flying a "P 47" in the ETO, Allen stayed in the Air Force for 20 more years before we met again at a high school reunion about 29 years later.

Not anxious to test my luck or the sentries a second time that morning, I sat out the rest of the night on a 30th Street station bench. Grabbing a few winks before "sun up", I managed to climb the Spruce Street fence and crawl in through an open dorm window. And plenty of time for early morning muster and calisthenics.

CHAPTER VII.

"ADMIRAL HALSEY AT SAGAMI WAN"

In April 1946 the U.S. Senate approved a committee recommendation to keep eight Five Star U.S. Officers on active duty for life. And, on May 13, 1946 at the Navy Department, the Judge Advocate General swore in Admiral William F. Halsey as a permanent Five Star Admiral. "My only fear", Halsey wrote to a friend "is that the extra stripe is going to interfere with my drinking arm".

Only months before..., on September 1, 1945, under the direction of the ship's gunnery officer..., a rehearsal of the Japanese surrender ceremony was held by 300 of the crew of the battleship U.S.S. Missouri. The next day it would be the duty of each man to escort the person that he was assigned to represent at rehearsal to the spot on the deck where he was to sit or stand during the historic surrender ceremony.

In recognition of his extraordinary contribution to the United States "split forces" fight with the Japs, on that day Admiral Halsey stood between General MacArthur and Admiral Forrest Sherman and immediately behind Admiral Nimitz's chair when Nimitz signed the surrender document for the United States.

At the conclusion, MacArthur leaned over and whispered to Halsey, "Start' em now!" "Aye Aye Sir!" And with that reply, the Admiral gave a "thumbs up" prearranged signal to an alerted staff officer to order the distant orbiting Army and Navy planes to head for Tokyo Bay to "fly over" the Missouri and the Third Fleet at anchor.

Only 5 days earlier, on August 29, 1945, Halsey's log read, "Steaming into Tokyo Bay, COMTHIRDFLEET in Missouri. Anchored at 0925 in Berth F71". Halsey would remember that date and time, "For forty five years my career in the United States Navy had been building toward that moment. Now those years were fulfilled and justified".

On the day before..., on the 28th.., the Jap representatives had gone aboard the Missouri to receive their surrender orders. And they were given fairly uncomplicated instructions. All Japanese gun positions were to fly a white flag..., and an individual with a key was to be visibly available for all buildings (from first hand experience, I believe that the Japs took this to mean that all doors were to be unlocked). And they were to have their emissaries show up to sign the surrender documents by 0900 on the 2nd. It should be noted that all instructions were meticulously followed.

In the Okinawa action, only several months before, the losses for the Navy were greater than any other major fleet action during the war — 30 ships sunk, more than 300 damaged and more than 12,500 killed, missing or wounded. American casualties on the island totalled 23,000 killed and 73,634 wounded. And 24,000 Okinawa civilians had died along with 99,000 of the 110,000 defending Japanese troops. Nevertheless, a number of officers concluded that the Jap was so badly beaten that they would elect to accept reality. An invasion of the homeland islands would not be necessary.

Many were doubtful, however, and, Admiral Ernest J. King and others (among them Admiral Halsey), with the responsibility of long years of experiencing Japanese tenacity, planned Operation Olympic (the invasion of Kyushu) for late October 1945 and Operation Coronet (Honshu) for March 1946. The anticipation of those operations provoked much discussion and speculation by Pacific personnel. Intensive training was proceeding, stores and equipment were being assembled, and new ships and crews were arriving to supplement the invasion fleet. The target date for "D Day" was only weeks away!

Admiral Richmond Kelly "Terrible" Turner, Commander of the Navy's Pacific Amphibious Forces, along with General MacArthur's deputy, General Eichelberger, determined that the Jap resistance would be so ferocious that it would take three Underwater Demolition Teams for each section of the Amphibious landing "beach head". Commander Draper Kauffman, Operational Planning "CO" for Underwater Demolition Teams, revealed after the war that the plan was to send in an initial three teams anticipating them to be wiped out. Follow up with another three teams; and then repeat it again with three more teams. Anticipating casualties making the first six teams non-operational, the reconnaissance and beach demolition and preparation would be finished by the last three teams. An estimated two-thirds overall casualties for the UDTs.

And undoubtedly, the 62 year old Halsey was the Admiral that would lead the anticipated final Pacific assault, an operation that experienced Pacific hands contemplated would cost a million casualties.

In October 1942, as operations turned increasingly in favor of the Japanese, the struggle for Guadalcanal had reached a bloody and unfavorable climax. At that point, a fighting Vice Admiral William F. Halsey arrived in the Solomon Islands. Relieving a dispirited U.S. South Pacific Command on orders from Pacific Headquarters at Pearl Harbor, in the next thirty remarkable days and nights of some of the most important naval exchanges with the Japs in WWII, Halsey reversed the tide of the Solomon Island campaign. And for the first time, the enemy was thrown on the defensive.

Although on December 7, 1941.. , by then a Vice Admiral.. , Halsey had served more than 41 years in the Navy, few Americans were acquainted with his name. But, by the Spring of 1946, it was Fleet Admiral Halsey, and he had become the most famous living Naval figure of his time.

But on December 7th, 1941, when Yamamoto's carriers were approaching Pearl Harbor by way of the "great circle" route, Halsey was at sea aboard the Big "E"... , the "Enterprise". The 59 year old "soon to be famous" Vice Admiral (born October 30, 1882), commanding Task Force 8, having been split off from TF 2, and comprised of the carrier Enterprise (Commanded by Captain George D. Murray), along with three heavy cruisers and nine destroyers, had raced to deliver Marine Fighters to Wake Island. Always apprehensive when it came to the Japanese, earlier Halsey had issued Battle Order No. 1 which started with;

1. The Enterprise is now operating under war conditions.
2. Any time, day or night, we must be ready for instant action.
3. Hostile submarines may be encountered............. .

When reading the orders, Halsey's operations officer, Commander William H. Buracker, was incredulous. And asked, "Admiral, did you authorize this?" And when Halsey replied in the affirmative, he questioned, "do you realize that this means war?" And then told the Admiral, "you can't start a private war of your own.... , who's going to take the responsibility?" Halsey replied, "I'll take it.. , we'll shoot first and argue afterwards!"

Halsey had loyal admirers and friends in the most obscure channels of the Navy. Though it is thought that Halsey was merely well informed, for his entire career, he had been openly skeptical of the Japanese. How well had he been informed at the time?

Along with "Lexington", both having just delivered Marine fighters to Wake Island, the carriers were returning separately to Pearl Harbor while it was still under attack. There were no carriers at Pearl on the 7th.

Referred to by the President as the mythical "Shangri-La" in order to conceal her identity, the brand new "Hornet", having been fitted out at Newport News, Virginia, was soon to complete it's "shake down". Commissioned the past October, just before December 7th, for her first mission, under Halsey, she would carry Army Airforce Colonel Jimmy Doolittle's pilots and 15 B-

25's to their launch point which turned out to be 800 miles East of Japan. It was from the "Hornet's" flight deck that the history making bombing run, often referred to as the "30 seconds over Tokyo", originated. Still at San Diego that December Sunday morning, requested by Halsey, the "Saratoga" was rushed immediately to Pearl Harbor. And by late December, pushing ahead their departure, the Chief of Naval Operations sent the new battleships, "North Carolina" and "Washington" heading out to the Pacific at "flank" speed.

Having graduated 43rd in a class of 63 on February 2, 1904, the 59 year old Halsey was about to write new complexities for modern Naval Warfare.

By the Fall of 1945, the old sailor, with the bushy eyebrows and famous grin that never quit in the face of unyielding pressure, had become revered and legendized by the officers and enlisted men of the wartime Navy.

As an ardent admirer, a 19-year old "eager to serve with Halsey" Midshipman at the University of Notre Dame at South Bend, Indiana, I first heard of the Scouts and Raiders and the Naval Combat Demolition Teams when an urgent request for "extra hazardous duty volunteers" was posted on the bulletin board on the fourth deck of formidable old Walsh Hall.

Having experienced the assignments of standing "deck watches" on the U.S.S. Wilmette and the "crash boats", Charlie 63 and 64 on Lake Michigan... , I knew that type of duty ... , standing watches aboard ship... , was not the way to vent one's wrath at the Jap. Much more preferable.., and at a much closer range, the place to be was right up on the beaches. As a matter of interest, commissioned in 1920, the U.S.S. Wilmette had the post WWI assignment of sinking the German U-Boat UC 97 in gunnery practice in about 185 feet of water about 16 miles off Wilmette, Illinois, a Northern suburban of Chicago. The "U" Boat, having operated in the North Sea during World War I.. , had been responsible for sinking seven Allied ships. After having helped to sell Victory Bonds.. , under the provisions of the Versailles Treaty, she was sunk on June 7, 1921 with 13 non-explosive shells from Wilmette's three inch deck gun.

In August 1943, when FDR and his party arrived in Georgian Bay for the Quebec Conference with Prime Minister Churchill and his party, they found the USS Wilmette waiting to provide communications capability to the outside world. And Wilmette's boats were used by the visiting Administration and Military Officials to fish in McGregory and Whitefish Bays.

With wooden decks to "holy stone", hammocks for sleeping (over the mess table area), a manual 3 inch 50 deck gun* and manual 20 MM and 40 MM's for gunnery practice, watches on the "bridge" and "flag bag", "general quarters" drills, and learning to cope with the rough "green" water of Lake Michigan, as always the Navy had not left a stone unturned to develop "seagoing" Midshipmen and provide them with sailor's "sea legs".

Same slow firing gun on deck 20 years after sinking UC 97.

To a young sailor, the stories of Admiral William F. "Bull" Halsey were awe inspiring. His blunt and colorful utterings from time to time, as to what his intentions were for the fate of Tojo, Yamamoto, and Hirohito.. , made them ours as well. Continuously documented, the Jap's less than "Frank Merriwell" fairness doctrine, and their well established brutality of Allied POWs (i.e. the Bataan Death March, Wake Island, Corregidor, Burma, Singapore, and Guadalcanal), drove many of those sailors to reflect on the attempts to discredit those Americans who had fought for the honor of their country. Honor, for which their forefathers, as every basic history class schoolboy knew, had paid a huge price in earlier American crises.

Typical of an early American family history beginning well before the Revolution, as a young boy I listened attentively to stories of my grandfather (wounded at Fredericksburg) and his brothers and of their incredible service at Gettysburg, Marketplace, Antietam, Bull Run, and White Oak Swamp. And others as they fought up and down the Shenendoah Valley with the Army of the Potomac under General George McClelland. Of Charles, my grandfather's brother, wounded and left for dead at Fredericksburg before being incarcerated at Andersonville and Libby prisons. And who later became the first post war Congressman from Florida. And John, their younger brother, shot in the neck and killed at Petersburg, the last battle of the war. Not abolitionists, their's was an outspoken dedication to fight to preserve the Union.. . Creating a history for all time... , their legacy left an indelible impression on that young boy.

When they "posted" the "UDT" and "Scouts and Raiders" request for volunteers on the fourth deck of Walsh Hall at Notre Dame.. , my Penn roommate and I immediately liked the sound of "Scouts and Raiders". And just the mention of "top secret.. extra hazardous duty" piqued a "Gung Ho" enthusiasm. Before my ex-roommate changed his mind, we had been the first to sign up to be interviewed. Responding with a sworn commitment to the interviewer, Commander Eacho.. , the information gained from that interview was classified.

As it happened, the friend from Penn days made a decision that it did not appeal to him. Opting out, he would eventually become an LCT "skipper".

Soon after, those volunteering, still not advised of their selection, were asked to meet privately with the Executive Officer,

Commander T. C. Scaffe, U.S. Navy (Ret.).   Explaining that "Scouts and Raiders" were being phased out, Scaffe went about the business of persuading those Midshipmen to switch allegiance and volunteer for "Naval Combat Demolition Units"... , "NCDUs".

As Ensigns, those chosen reported to "Navy Combat Demolition Training and Experimental" camp at Fort Pierce, Florida.

Very young and impressionable, these men went to work with many dedicated UDT officers... , men like Commander Jack T. Koehler, Draper L. Kauffman, T.C. Crist, L.A. States, Tom Flynn, John Horrocks and lots more. Those men were in their mid 20s to early 30s. But, to a 19-20 year old Ensign, came across somber beyond their years.

A particular hero to many, beginning early in the war.., from the time that he carried off the raid on Tokyo with Colonel Jimmy Doolittle and the carrier Hornet "task group", Admiral William F. Halsey told us what he would do to the Japs... And what was printed was only the published version of his expressed intentions for the enemy.

When the tide was running hard against the United States and the Navy, Halsey gave the whole country a boost by announcing his intention of riding the Emperor's white horse through Tokyo. And then, as C.O. of the Third Fleet, "set about" to blast his way across the Pacific to find the Emperor's horse. To show the country their enthusiastic support for Halsey, the Chamber of Commerce of Reno, Nevada sent him a silver and jeweled saddle. And the Lions Club of Montrose, Colorado, eagerly added a bridle, blanket and lariat.

Having somehow "shanghaied" a mascot on Maui, UDT 22 made clandestine plans to get him aboard ship... . And then honored him in a more pragmatic fashion.. , naming their mongrel after the Commander of the ubiquitous 3rd Fleet... "Winched" aboard in a sea bag, "Halsey" enjoyed much respect and affection from the UDT's as well as the ship's crew.

"Halsey" (the dog), last seen chasing German POWs at Coronado Island in November 1945 at the time the team was being decommissioned, could now have a descendent? Perhaps named "Wolfgang", and a mascot to one of today's Navy Seal Teams.

But in those war years, it was a big, big Navy and the Pacific theater of war included.. , even by today's communication and fleet standards.. , an incredible geographical area. Whenever the Fleet assembled.. , Ulithi Atoll, Sagami Wan, Kwajalein.. , carriers and battle ships were anchored in lines never seen before or since. Many of the legendary names.. , Iowa, Wisconsin, Pennsylvania, North Carolina, North Dakota, "The Big E", Grayback, Tang, Franklin, Indianapolis... were yet to tell their story. Just inside the gate of the Philadelphia Navy Yard following the war… , opposite the Officer's Club, was a similar reminder of those dangerous times. A row of decommissioned Heavy Cruisers, names that made incredible history in the Pacific War, were tied up and mothballed there for many years. Before they gradually disappeared, having been sent to foreign navies or scrapped, there were quiet and sentimental reflecting moments for a legion of sailors passing that lineup of gray warriors.., all cocooned and battened down…, some forever.

As with thousands of others, our duty in September 1945 placed us "on the spot" when the final drama was to unfold.

Even before MacArthur, and the 11th Airborne Division, landed at Atsugi Airfield (near Tokyo), the UDTs had assisted in securing, among other installations, the big Yokosuka Naval Base. And at Atsugi.., to greet MacArthur.., compliments of the UDTs and other Navy units (several took credit), was a large sign that read, "Welcome U.S. ARMY.. , The Third Fleet". And in Yokosuka, UDTs boarded the heavily damaged, burned and blackened "Nagato". After ordering the ship's Captain to strike the battleship's colors, the "Stars and Stripes" were run up to take their place.

The only Japanese battleship afloat after four years of war, in 1941 "Nagato" had served as the flagship of Admiral Isoroku Yamamoto. On board at the time of the sneak Pearl Harbor raid, the crafty Admiral planned and directed the attack from the battleship's wardroom while the ship lay at anchor close to shore in quiet Sagami Wan waters off Yokosuka. Pacing her bridge on that fateful December 7th, Yamamoto received one pilot's electrifying transmission… , "tora tora tora!"…, "surprise achieved". The first battleship to be armed with 16 inch guns, it has been said that "Nagato" added another dimension at Pearl Harbor. Since some of Yamamoto's carrier aircraft were equipped with Nagato's 16 inch shells, especially modified to be dropped as bombs., some are convinced that it was one of those shells that sank the battleship U.S.S. Arizona. If true.., then the Nagato was repayed! Taken to Bikini, and blasted in the first "Atomic Bomb" test after the war, today she lies upside down at the bottom of Bikini Atoll with her four massive screws sticking straight up and covered by growing coral heads and surrounded by other colorful undersea life.

Evidencing extensive damage inflicted by Halsey's raids, beginning as early as the B-25 attack in early 1942, and ending with the "at will" forays by the Third Fleet in August 1945, the Marines took up positions on the perimeters of the Yokosuka base soon after going ashore. Up until the surrender ceremony, they held only the perimeters until the occupation forces could be built up.

In the event the Jap "die hards" on Honshu had successfully pulled off their planned coup, that "toe hold" would have been crucial to the occupation.

Then, with the Third Fleet at anchor and a "condition watch" set, alerted to retaliate in the event that the Kamikaze spirit was not completely subdued... , the foreordained dreaded moment for the Japs came when they met with MacArthur, Nimitz, Halsey and Wainwright.

MacArthur, after a brief twenty seven minutes, tersely dismissed the Japanese and closed the ceremony. After an hour of coffee and doughnuts in the Missouri's wardroom.. , the Flag Group began to disperse... There was much to do.

It can only be surmised.. , that by then the old Navy gold braid had begun to enthusiastically enjoy the occasion.... A moment in time that had literally taken their lifetime to achieve. Nothing even slightly similar will ever occur again.

Someone at the top... , a Nimitz.. Turner.. Halsey.. Wilkinson.. Sherman.. , must have suggested "going ashore". As Sailors usually express it, to "pitch a little liberty". Just as the lowest Seaman 2nd... , they also had to be curious to take a look at these bastards that had taken a big chunk out of what should have been the less demanding years of their lives. And disrupted or cut short the life of friends, and shipmates.

And where does a Naval Officer.., at a naval installation.., no matter what part of the world, head for first when he knows of no place else to go? Of course.. , to the closest Officers' Club.

The Yokosuka Officers' Club was a beat up... , shell of a concrete building. Like the entire Jap Naval Base, it retained the smell of death... , an indescribable stench.

As dimly recalled, the place had hardly any real furniture. At one end, in the inevitable center of activity, was a long low fixture that some mess attendants had turned into a bar. But the large room consisted mostly of a lot of open space with very odd and archaic restrooms. Like most buildings in Japan in those days, at least for Americans, the "overhead" was very low. Evidently at a height to accommodate the small stature of most Japanese. Within a few days the Commander of the Third Fleet began to allow a few officers to go ashore within the confines of the Yokosuka Naval Base. And the large room, which comprised the Officer's Club, became filled with all types of interesting "Pacific" characters..... There were some pretty salty hats and nothing but worn and faded khakis. The "uniform of the day" called for "no ties"... , none were evident.

Apparently the Navy saw fit to allow small numbers of Jap "policemen" and maintenance workers to work around the outside of the building. Inside the club, only U.S. Navy Stewards

Mates served as bartenders. Typical books of Officer Club "chits" were sold. And prices were pretty fair, you could buy a couple of fingers of "Haig and Haig Pinch Bottle" scotch, with a splash of soda, for 15 cents. Served in glasses from bottles displayed on the very low bar, the best labels of liquor were plentiful. Made cold in ice and water filled tubs, for 10 cents, those with a thirst for beer, were handed wet brown bottles of Pacific "3.2". There was absolutely no food available... , not even a peanut. And the Japs in attendance may have been what they said they were... , "policemen" and "maintenance workers".. . But, in retrospect, wearing parts of old uniforms, it seemed obvious that they were more than that. Even in devastating defeat, the usual Japanese deviousness continued.

Not particularly friendly, they were openly cooperative and all saluted or bowed when passing. Except for those mentioned, who apparently had been specially chosen for that duty on the Yokosuka base, initially the city streets were almost deserted. It was later revealed that government radio had warned their citizens to expect waves of rape and pillaging. Just as their forces had been known to commit in Nanking and other Chinese cities.

Surprised by their sudden and unexpected surrender, and curious to attain some insight as to Japanese thinking and viewpoint, an attempt to communicate was made on a number of occasions. Seemingly more often than anticipated, at least superficially, they attempted unsuccessfully to appear friendly. Speaking excellent English, several of those on base acknowledged having attended college in California. At least one of them had claimed the University of California at Berkley as his Alma Mater. Considering their appearance and the circumstances..., and my narrow subjective concept, this came as a startling surprise. Coming from a very provincial youth in Pennsylvania..., and meeting Japanese who over a half a century earlier had gone all the way to the States for their education in that pre-WWII period, is as baffling today as it was then.

An unconvinced skeptic when it comes to the Japanese... , it would be my assumption that an education in the States had been orchestrated by the Japanese Military establishment. A military, with it's 1930's successes in China, that provoked it to anticipate the same results in their war with the Americans.

Before going ashore that warm day in September 1945, UDT officers were made aware of the scuttlebutt concerning the Officer's Club. Just as with "top brass".. , the UDT Officers also headed for the former Japanese club. And were joined by two shipmates, the very companionable ship's Doctor, Lieutenant Robert P. Jessup, USNR, and another ship's officer, whose titles included ship's "First Lieutenant" and "Damage Control Officer", Lieuten-

ant Charles B. Fisackerly, USNR. A "mustang", or former
enlisted man, who had spent most his war in the Pacific,
Fisackerly was one of the most experienced of the APD's officer
complement. Their shipboard functions, having brought them
more directly in contact with the UDT operation, both officers
were regularly involved and closer to UDT personnel. "Ships
company", aboard tiny crowded APDs, were not reputed to have
an over friendly relationship with the UDTs. And in this particular instance, the situation was aggravated by the Executive
Officer, an overbearing New York City native, whose resentment
of having UDTs aboard was conspicuously overt. And eminently
recognized and criticized by other ship's officers.

The UDTs were painfully aware that the King George V, a
Royal Navy Battleship, and the pride and joy of the Brits, had
anchored a few hundred yards away. Aware!! Every afternoon
the George's signal bridge ran up the "splice the main brace"
pennant. And shortly after that, the "limeys" could enjoy their
"pints".... Something that was, and still is, "off limits" to sailors
in the United States Navy.

Even the Ship's Doctor.. , whose medical supplies included a
substantial supply of Leigion Brandy in those miniature bottles...,
could not partake. However, during the various reconnaissance
and landing operations in the process of "securing" Japan... ,
UDT personnel did, on a number of occasions, sample the ship's
brandy supply. Returning to the ship from a reconnaissance in
the hostile, dirty, and cold waters off Honshu and Kyushu,
handed out by the "Doc", they were downed straight. No chaser!

But at the Yokosuka Officer's Club, and on their first liberty in
some time, and with some hefty drinks.. , and no food, the two
APD officers soon began to contemplate their inconclusive recent
career. Suddenly, faced with a future that had not been expected
to occur so rapidly, and for which there had been little planning,
at the time the surrender was viewed with some apprehension.
Something comparable to suddenly being told that you were
being "laid off".

And facing the possibility of being unemployed in a world
crowded with millions of others in the same circumstances.
Expecting to meet and decisively defeat the Japs in a "face off" on
the beaches of Kyushu and Honshu, until August 1945, the most
realistic timetable was usually expressed in the then optimistic
slogan "GOLDEN GATE IN `48". In other words, only three more
years in the Pacific.

It seems that there was always a lot of singing along the way
in the Pacific... , sometimes with a great deal of nostalgia. And
in the Fall of '45, some Navy man put together some new words
to a popular WWII tune that seemed to describe the sudden

change in their game plan. Considering the events that had taken place, a little less optimistic ditty sung to the tune of the sentimentally popular World War II song "*ALWAYS*".... :
I'll be oversees..., ALWAYS... .
Standing O.O.D.'s..., ALWAYS... .
(ref. Officer of the deck watch)
When the things we've planned....
Need a helping hand....
I'll be in Japan..., ALWAYS..., ALWAYS...,

When they count the score..., ALWAYS...,
I'll need ten points more..., ALWAYS...,
(reference to the discharge point system)

Not for just for now... ,
Not for just for then... ,
But I'll be in Japan... , ALWAYS... , AlWAYS..>>>>>>.
Not distracted.. , laughing and completely involved in their own conversation, the APD shipmates were in "fine fettle" as they started down the hill toward the officer's "liberty boat" landing. Anchored far out along side some of the "heaviest hitters" of Halsey's Third Fleet, the APD sent it's small boats (LCPRs) on scheduled regular ship to shore runs. To provide surveillance and reaction to potential underwater attacks by reported suicide swimmers, as a precaution, the "Young" had been ordered to anchor next to the Navy's newest and last battleship, the 45,000 ton Missouri. Ships, that comprised the Navy's hurriedly plotted Sagami Wan anchorage, had filled to capacity those recently hostile Jap waters. And easily visible to the West of the anchored Third Fleet, like a classical photograph out of our grade school Geography books, or the centerfold of National Geographic, the snow capped Mount Fujiyama stood serenely alone in front of the setting sun.

Along with the less than "steady as you go" course of these two celebrating APD Officers... , their "stop start" progress was further interrupted by their penchant for meeting and swapping "sea stories" with each new Navy friend encountered along the way.

Not successful in encouraging an increase in their deliberate pace... , their plodding headway toward the boat landing almost insured they would not be in time to make the next liberty boat.

Allowing plenty of time for short side trips to explore the various buildings and installations along the way, a recently "downed" and burned carrier plane.. , an "SBD" Dauntless, was discovered and checked out. The spectacle of the burned plane, and particularly the uncertain fate of the pilot, recalled regularly over the past 50 years, naturally detracted from the lightness of the occasion. Also of interest were the many inoperable anti-aircraft guns tucked away in all sorts of niches. And the numerous midget submarines (kaitens) and suicide boats had already been put out of commission by the UDTs. After leaving a gymnasium type building used by Jap officers to practice Jujitsu, I checked to undertake to insure that my two APD friends were making progress toward the boat landing.

Checking another "bombed out" building, intending to again check on the progress of the two Lieutenants, I walked out of the dark building and became temporarily blinded by the bright Fall sunlight. It took only a second to get my relative bearing. But I blinked a lot more when the first thing that caught my attention was a seemingly huge entourage of portly men in khakis, "gold braid", rapidly moving up the hill.... Heading in my direction..., straight ahead in their path..., were the two APD "shipmates".

Laughing and conversing as they moved directly ahead, their destination was obviously the Officers' Club at the top of the hill. The junior "flags" followed bringing up the rear. There must have been forty in the party, almost all Flag Rank, with the three or four easily recognizable Admirals taking the lead. It widened gradually before tailing off at the rear. Prominently recognizable were the unmistakable smiling Admirals Nimitz and Halsey. In disbelief, one young sailor was stopped dead in his tracks.

Straight ahead..., in front of Admirals Halsey and Nimitz..., and closing fast..., were two of the "happiest" and "luckiest" to ever have conquered Japan. Appearing to be completely oblivious to the situation, ostensibly in the middle of enjoying what must have been a hilarious joke. Or it may be it was their dubious reaction to all that "gold braid" rapidly bearing down on them. On a "collision" course, the prospect of having to navigate around that phalanx would have "boggled" any Pacific sailor.

Admiral Halsey.., the "Senior Operating Officer Present" (SOOP)..., out in front and his immediate boss at his side, apparently felt compelled to personally take charge of the situation. And that he did!

While the entire "Flag" contingent stopped dead in their tracks, no longer smiling, Halsey alone continued to steadily move on course to confront the two, suddenly withering, shipmates. With his reputation for down to earth "sailor ways", obviously experienced with that sort of thing, Halsey was in his element and quickly threw them on the defensive. "What ship sailor? Making it clear that he was not unsympathetic, he quietly mentioned his concern. Lowering his voice, barely heard, he very forcefully ordered..., "Lieutenants, return to your ship at once."

Turning his back on the "still at attention" APD shipmates..., the old Admiral's unmistakable famous wide grin most likely reflected his private thoughts. Seemingly noticing me for the first time, he turned in my direction. Having been engrossed in interviewing Japs, exploring the Yokosuka Naval Base, looking for souvenirs... , and having only consumed two bottles of 3.2 Navy issue beer.. , I was cold sober.

From the time the "brass" entourage was first spotted, I had remained at rigid attention.. , at "hand salute". And was more surprised, a little relieved, when the Admiral, returning my salute, addressed me with that never ending Halsey smile. In typical Navy parlance, "Good afternoon Ensign..., what ship?" "Underwater Demolition", Sir!

Then throwing in, "same ship as the others", his smile didn't quite completely fade. Then he barely whispered, "see that your shipmates get back to the ship". Snapping off another salute, "Aye Aye Sir"!

This time, I was amazed to see both Nimitz and Halsey... , and most of the others, return the salute.

Exchanging a quick glance with Nimitz... looking back at the others, Halsey's entire entourage started forward as if on command. After long Naval careers, coping with the Japanese always hovering on the horizon, here they were in the No.1 Jap Naval Officers' Club... , such as it was. And not as invited guests! And certainly would have preferred to be going to the "Top of the Mark"... , a Navy hangout that Halsey enjoyed in San Francisco. Nevertheless, headed for what had to be a private "moment in time" for them as well... , a few drinks to toast a hard won victory.

But the three luckless "part timers", finally arriving back at the landing, discovered that they had just missed their "liberty boat". It meant waiting at least several hours until the last scheduled trip of the day could return them to their APD.

Sitting around listening to the monotonous steady slap of Sagami Wan waves... , when the "LCPR" still did not arrive, my shipmates were becoming increasingly irritable... . Instead, a handsome Admiral's barge came smartly along side. Striking up a conversation, we quickly learned that it was the Barge of Admiral Theodore (Ping) Wilkinson. And that the Admiral had given the crew very specific orders as to what time he should be picked up... , 1800. And sure enough, at 1800 "on the dot", punctual in the tradition of an accepted centuries old military legacy, the three star Admiral suddenly appeared. By that time, having grown tired and slowly showing signs of sobering.. , my shipmates became increasingly dejected and even repentant. But mostly tired!   The Admiral commanded the now famous Third Amphibious Fleet.., of which we sometimes claimed membership. Not letting our "tired" show, we managed a little military bearing to muster the old "amphibious salute".

Wasting no time boarding his barge, we waited to see who would give the orders to the coxswain to "shove off". When abruptly he turned and asked, "what ship sailor?" "APD Young"..., repeating the reply given Halsey. Conferring with his Bos'n, he turned to simply offer to take us out to the ship.

No hesitation... , we were happy to accept this unprecedented offer. And immediately boarded the covered barge for, as I recall, about a half hour run. That tells a little bit about the size of the anchorage. Underway.., the Admiral's steady conversation acknowledged that earlier he had been with the Nimitz and Halsey party at the Yokosuka Officers' Club. Although never mentioned, I knew that we were recognized by our earlier exchange with Admiral Halsey. And vividly recall our discussion and agreement concerning the musty stench... , seemingly in all of Japan... , not just from the Officers' Club... . Making us both anxious to get out of there fast. Unsaid, it was unmistakably clear that all hands were happy to be getting back to the sanitation of the ship.

When it came time to weigh anchor, to finally leave Japan, I never looked back. An old Navy custom suggests that throwing a few coins over the side, as a good luck offering upon departure from a foreign port, will bring the thrower back for a future happy visit. In this case, I would save myself a few coins.

Arriving back at the "Young".. , paying our compliments and expressing our appreciation to Admiral Wilkinson, we boarded the APD. Saluting the colors and the "Officer of the Deck", the three of us proceeded directly to the ward room where the Steward on duty had fresh black coffee. And there was a pineapple topped sheet cake right out of the galley oven. As pervasive as Australian mutton, pineapple was served in and on everything.

A great experience but, tainted just a trifle by the conflict of the rules of commissioned conduct and the individual exuberances at the time, not to be divulged to shipmates. Discussing that liberty was deliberately avoided. And after a week or two, in private discussions recalling the incident, the details gradually became a little more clear-cut. And relived over and over again by those involved before the UDTs left the ship at Coronado, . Now that encounter is remembered rather matter of factly, only a tiny "sidebar" vignette in an overall historic surrender mural. As also was the case of the famous Admirals.. , Halsey, Nimitz and Wilkinson.. , this was the way we were to conclude that chapter in our wartime experience. How many encounters like that one did Halsey have in Japan? In WWII? In his entire career? How many Japanese officers clubs had he visited? German? Italian?

British? Canadian? Not a typical page out of the life of a WWII sailor, this amusing episode... , contributes a little humor to a significant historical event.

Remarkably, only a few days later, after the Marine perimeter was extended beyond the Yokosuka base, Bill Collins, a 3rd platoon officer, and I, unexpectedly encountered another of the most famous military figures of the 20th century. Coming out of his new quarters in the Imperial Hotel in downtown Tokyo, we were surprised to photograph General Douglas MacArthur climbing into the back seat of his old pre-war black Cadillac. Along with lots of interesting MacArthur and World War II memorabilia, that same Cadillac may now be seen in the Douglas MacArthur Museum located in the former Norfolk Court House.

Early in 1946, in another unusual twist, with Headquarters located only a few doors from the then County Court House, I was assigned to the Fifth Naval District Shore Patrol at Norfolk, Virginia. And I visited the Court house for the first time 45 years later when it contained the General Douglas MacArthur Museum.

There is also the tragic "George Patton like" sequel to the Yokosuka incident involving Admiral Wilkinson. Upon returning to Coronado, having decommissioning the UDT, I reported for duty at the Naval Gun Factory in Washington, D.C.. With the newly "beefed up" Atlantic Fleet under Admiral Jonas Ingram, CIC, and the brand new Eighth Fleet under Admiral Marc Mitscher, "home ported" at Norfolk, the Fifth Naval District was again about to be a very busy "liberty town".

Assigned to Navy Shore Patrol Headquarters early in 1946..., a radio dispatch was received from the scene indicating a Cadillac.., with an Admiral on board.. , had drifted off the bow of the Portsmouth Ferry. Responding instantaneously, recalling my prior UDT duty, the Duty Officer attempted to locate and direct me to the scene of the sunken automobile. Having been on duty all of the previous night, I was half way between the Court Street "SP" Headquarters and my bunk at the enlisted barracks at City Park. No names were given, and not knowing the occupants, I hit the siren and headed for the ferry slip by the shortest route.

"Ping" Wilkinson's body was recovered immediately, but it was too late to save the life of the Admiral..., my friend from Yokosuka... . Though a big man, dragged down and trapped by his heavy wet "bridge coat", his body was quickly pulled to the surface. And, eventually the car also was recovered. Over the years, I have privately agonized over the incident again and again. The "what if" scenario.. . If only I had hung around a few more minutes and been there when the initial call came in... , or I might have been closer to the scene... , maybe worked an extra

15 minutes etc....... .

Those who are familiar with the story... will readily recall that.. , before he drowned, the gallant Admiral Wilkinson managed to open the passenger's door and shove his wife out. And saved her life!.

And that's how I recall that afternoon in September 1945..., only a few hours after the formal Japanese Surrender.. . That brief encounter with Bill Halsey.. , one of only a few heroes in my life time.. , held no surprises. He was exactly as any WWII sailor would have expected.

For many years, I have read and appreciated the numerous documented biographical sketches of Admiral Halsey.. , his greatness., and most of all his very human qualities. Unlike Douglas MacArthur, he was not academically first in his class and, as a Midshipman, he had his vulnerabilities and share of youthful escapades that brought criticism from his superiors and sometimes his peers. Born on October 30, 1882, he was just 63 in the Fall of 1945. And yet he was very much in touch with the young sailors of his fleet. As a Senior Naval Officer, according to scuttlebutt, he could pitch a "Navy liberty" that can only be appreciated by one that has been there.... And, as a junior officer, he was no stranger to a little "hack time". Although he often did not conform with others in high places, the many criticisms of his inspiring rhetoric, and aggressive leadership, during the darkest days of the war, reflected on his powerful strength of character.

Admiral Halsey exemplified, at the highest level, General George Marshall's often spoken credo:

"If one can't disobey an order, he'll never amount to much of a leader".

And in his bold and inspiring leadership, in the face of overwhelming odds, he exemplified Admiral Arleigh "30 knott" Burke, who has often been quoted as saying, "Any Commander who fails to exceed his authority is not much use to his subordinates".

And now, as over 50 years have passed... , when I want to lose myself in those nostalgic recollections of faded khakis.. , and remember the constantly soaked sand shoes that became molded to our feet.. , my thoughts instinctively return to that craggy face and wide smile under the incredibly bushy eyebrows.

Reminded of the ominous uncertainty of those days in the sea and sun.. , as only one who has lived them can fathom.. , a quiet harbor of invulnerability is to immerse myself in those years with the stories of the life and times of Admiral William F. "Bull" Halsey.

CHAPTER VIII.

"Letters To Home and... , Admissions"

"the tactical handling of the U.S. Fifth Fleet... , the armada which carried the assault force to Okinawa... , and set it down so successfully..., was nothing short of brilliant. The logistical support of the great fleet at sea over a protracted period was unprecedented, and a most remarkable demonstration of efficiency....."

As a result of some 1942 foresight of the Navy Department, the build up of the forces that contributed to the final destruction of the Pacific enemy was well represented by a corps of "Red and Blue" junior officers. Imbued with a character of discipline, as wartime will inevitably and imperiously instill... , their training resulted in their rapid evolvement into military professionals.

Represented by growing numbers as the count down to final offensives intensified, they sweated out the liberation of the Phillipines.... And, regarded to be strategic to the final offensive against the home islands, participated in the capture of a tiny barren 8 square mile volcanic ash island. Built by Navy "CBs", new runways on Iwo Jima provided a safe landing for crews of "low on fuel" B-29s returning to the Marianas from incendiary raids over cities like Tokyo, Yokohama and Kobe on the Island of Honshu.

Penn sailors were frequently among crews manning the ships confronting the enemy in the costliest engagement in the United States' long contentious naval history. Coded "Operation Iceberg", historians have recorded...........;

"the tactical handling of the U.S. Fifth Fleet... , the armada which carried the assault force to Okinawa... , and set it down so successfully... , was nothing short of brilliant. The logistical support of the great fleet at sea over a protracted period was unprecedented, and a most remarkable demonstration of efficiency....."

Ready for whatever came their way, the sailors were prepared to dish it out! But there was an enormous cost in the expenditure of men and ships. The Commander in Chief of the Pacific Fleet, usually impassive in presenting his official battle report, was not unmoved when he later disclosed that 30 ships had been sunk, while 300 more had been damaged. Americans seem to readily recall that Iwo Jima was a costly operation and it was. But there were 12,500 Navy men killed and missing in the fight for Okinawa, twice the casualty rate of Iwo Jima. American casualties totalled 23,000 killed and 73,634 wounded. And 24,000 Okinawa civilians had died along with 99,000 of the 110,000 defending Japanese troops. And for the first time, Japanese troops, surrendering in large numbers, were shipped as prisoners to Guam and Hawaii.

Mostly flying down from Kyushu and Shikoku, 1465 Jap Kamikaze planes took part in day and night raids on the fleet operating off Okinawa. Piloted by fanatical untrained "one way" Kamikaze suicide pilots, from bases on the Southern most home islands of Kyushu and Shikoku, as their final act they had only one objective.., to sink a U.S. ship. Anxious to get the ordeal over with, most Kamikazes would attack the first ship encountered…, usually one on picket duty on the perimeter of the fleet. Uncoordinated, and arriving in bunches, frequently two or three would dive simultaneously on a single small ship.

During the most fierce period of those attacks, looking to devise an effective Kamikaze defense, Vice-Admiral Richmond Kelly Turner, Commander of the "Joint Expeditionary Force", recognized that the poorly trained pilots would commit at their first opportunity. And responded by deploying a screen of Destroyers (DDs) and Destroyer Transports (APDs) to protect his landing force.., of AKAs, APAs, LSTs, LSMs, LCIs, LCMs, LCTs, LSDs and similar and modified auxiliaries supporting the landing force ashore.

As the 5th Fleet stood off Okinawa throwing everything it had at the suicide pilots, by some unexplained communications quirk, the "TBS" (Talk Between Ships) silence was suddenly broken by the barely audible static choked voice of a young Ensign reporting on the status of the Kamikaze inflicted damage on his Destroyer. Along with others positioned on the perimeter of the great fleet, his "picket" was in the throes of beating back another attack by fanatical Jap pilots.

Barely underway, with only limited steerage, and without the use of the Mark 37 Director, he had continued to fight the ship with the two remaining 5 inch 38 calibre guns. Incredulously, all other ship's officers having been killed, the Ensign had survived to assume the command of his Destroyer.

Continuing his "on air" assessment for anyone who might be listening, the embattled young officer was remembered as saying, "I am an Ensign.., and although I have been aboard.., and in the Navy only a short time… , I will fight this ship the best that I can. Though I know that I shall make mistakes…………." The reception faded to static… , and then there was only silence.

Surrounded by the idiosyncratic sounds of battle, you could hear a pin drop within the confines of those "bridges" picking up that transmission. Abruptly cut off… , it is assumed, that the attack having been renewed, the Destroyer was one of those that would be reported lost. The identity or ultimate fate of the Ensign has never been established.

Why Okinawa? Denied permission by the Soviets to construct runways to "shuttle bomb" Honshu, as well as staging areas on the continent for the final amphibious assault.. , the Ryukyu Islands would be necessary to serve as a base to launch those final operations. Over 5000 miles from the U.S. shores.... , there were those that were doubtful concerning the cost of an amphibious assault in the magnitude of "Operation Olympic". But Admiral Ernest J. King, and others sharing the responsibility in those long years of experiencing Japanese tenacity (among them Admiral Halsey), went "flank speed" ahead with the amphibious operation (the attack on Kyushu) set for October 15th to November 1, 1945, and "Operation Coronet" (Honshu) for March 1946. The enormity of those operations whipped up much debate and speculation among Pacific operations experts. Nevertheless, intensive rehearsals were proceeding, stores and equipment were being assembled, and new ships and crews were arriving daily to supplement the invasion fleet.

Admiral Turner, expecting to command the amphibious forces, huddling with General MacArthur's deputy, General Eichelberger, and UDT Commander Draper Kauffman, determined that the Jap resistance would be so ferocious that it would take three Underwater Demolition Teams for each Amphibious landing "beach head". Anticipating 100 percent casualties in the first two teams on each beach, Kauffman estimated that it would add up to two-thirds overall casualties for the UDTs, the loss of six teams before the last three replacement teams could complete the operation.

No doubt about it, the invincible "Bull" Halsey was the right man to lead his "Third Fleet", in annihilating the Jap defenses and, in it's greatest victory. As the Jap resistance was expected to remain as fanatical as in the past, old Pacific hands predicted a million casualties.

And Penn men were in the thick of it when the U.S. and Australian forces took back "oil rich" Balikpapen from the entrenched Japs, before handing it back to their Dutch Allies.

More recently, at the time of the May 7th 50th Anniversary celebration of "VE" Day, Navy men were quick to react to incredulous statements made during the TV coverage of that event. Pacific veterans were particularly incensed by contemporary journalists, who hadn't even been born, persistently reporting that, "the war was over!" When, in fact, Fleet and ground forces action, with heavy losses in men and ships, had continued to rage for four more months. Right up until the September 2nd surrender.

A major disaster, among numerous losses, in that closing period before the final capitulation on September 2nd, the moving account of the Heavy Cruiser "Indianapolis" shook the Naval establishment all the way to Washington. In addition to Okinawa, participating in early Southwest Pacific action, at New Guinea, up in the Aleutians and back down to the Gilberts, then the Western Carolines, the Marshalls and the Marianas, it looked as if the old cruiser would survive the war.

With spacious "Admiral's country", for that reason it had been chosen by Admiral Raymond A. Spruance, Commander of the 5th Fleet, as his flagship. Even though the Cruiser's design was faulty to the extent that it had been predicted she would be unable to sustain even one torpedo, Spruance chose it any way for it's spacious and comfortable quarters.

Unescorted on that overcast night of July 31, 1945, the long time veteran of many Pacific operations was torpedoed by an enemy "sub" between Saipan and the Phillipines. Only 316 of the 1200 man crew survived in a shark infested sea.

The same weekend commemorating the "VE Day" anniversary, declaring himself to be a boy of six on that date, Winston Churchill, the grandson of Britons's esteemed wartime Prime Minister, vigorously proclaimed that the U.S. could never have been capable of invading the continent by itself. And, had not the British held firm, implied that the U.S. would still be subjected to government under the "swastika". It is doubtful that young (56 years of age) Churchill has ever heard a WWII American dispute the valor of his fellow countrymen. But his knowledge of the times seems to be a little narrow when it comes to U.S. power and perseverance in the Pacific Theater! He could not have given much consideration to the Navy's incredible logistics achievements. Though fighting a "split forces" war, alone the U.S. Fleet had planted U.S. ground forces on Japan's doorstep. While Tokyo, 5300 miles by the "great circle" route from San Francisco, is approximately 1500 miles further from the U.S.A. than the coast of France, Bordeaux is only 3800 miles from New York. The powerful and growing Fleet's floating logistical support, not only permitting it to operate and attack Japs at will... had also mastered the powerful support of overwhelming, never to be denied, amphibious forces.

And more evidence of sketchy knowledge of WWII history was exhibited by the pedantic conservative syndicated columnist George Will. Attributing his blundering opinion, during an appearance on the Sunday morning "David Brinkley" show, to the number of Russian casualties in WWII, he spluttered, "Russia won the war". From a reputed writer and scholar.. , student of history? An implausible statement!

Studies of the "Magic" (code breaker) "Diplomatic Summaries" disclose that General George Catlett Marshall confirmed early in the war that the Soviets would not cooperate, and join with the U.S.A. in it's fight with the Japs. Having been denied by Stalin to allow American land based air to support the Fleet from Russian soil, the U.S. had no choice but to fight costly island assaults across the South and Central Pacific. With priority given to the European Theater, with troops spread over all seven continents, the U.S. had fought a "split forces" war. Naval commanders in the Pacific, without priorities extended the ETO Command, were often shorted of ships.. , men.. , food.. , fuel.., and ammunition. There is no basis to young Churchill's argument that the U.S. would not have persevered without either Russia or Britain... .

Late in August 1945, the Third Fleet, commanded by Admiral Halsey, and the "Amphibs", led by Vice Admiral Kelly Turner, rolled into a bleak and almost deserted Sagami Wan. A few "Quaker Sailors", ashore to assist in securing the Jap's preeminent Naval base prior to September 2nd, witnessed from a distance the surrender ceremony aboard the Battleship U.S.S. Missouri at anchor not far from shore.

"Red and Blue" Sailors aboard ships anchored in the shadow of snow capped Mount Fujiyama, relaxing and "on hold" in the midst of an armada that extended as far as the eye could see, took the time to begin to ponder their return to the Quaker City campus. To escape from the atrocious odor of the bomb ravaged Honshu..., to again inhale the pungent smell of stale beer and musty peanut shells that forever cluttered the cellar floor of "Smokey Joe's" on 36th Street.. , to be awakened by the never ending "clanging" of trolleys edging slowly as they criss-crossed the 37th and Woodland intersection... , to "wind up" a long evening by scoffing three or four 10 cent hamburgers with the all night crowd at the "White Tower" opposite the Dorms... , to tread the shiny worn uneven floors... and crowded stairs... of stately Logan Hall... , to climb the steep front steps leading up to Logan's brownstone arched entrance and green serpentine stone walls... , to engage in an after dark impromptu tryst under the gaze of Edgar Fahs Smith, who, even today, remains pensively unbesmirched by all those witnessed lascivious liaisons in front of venerable old "Weightman".

To contemplate a reprieve from the fortress like somber ambience of 72 year old "Hare", by finagling a class or two in the fairly modern Bennett Hall at bustling 34th and Walnut.

Concerned that a "backlog" of returning "GI" applications would unduly postpone their readmittance, Quaker Sailors were busily forwarding free "V-Mail" requests to the Dean of Admissions. Though the fervor of war operations had subsided, the

Navy never stopped planning numerous operational diversions to support the occupation. While the Penn Men began to warm to the thought of trading worn khakis for soft "tweeds", "oxford button downs", and "white bucks", amphibious type operations continued to be required in order to deploy arriving troops. Deployed to such previously unfamiliar places as...., Aomori Bay, Niigata, Hokkaido, Fuchow, Sasebo, Formosa, Wonson, Pusan and Hakodate. Plus even a few of those familiar names studied in Miss Faber's 5th grade geography class..., Yokohama, Tokyo and Shanghai.

Days evolved into months. The tiny beginning trickle of ships and sailors returning to the U.S. gradually became a gushing torrent. Once ashore in California, they would face a long slow train jaunt across the country. With thousands of others disembarking from ships returning to the West Coast, they were confronted with "standing room only" ancient coaches packed with GIs determined to be in the East on Christmas Day.

New ship arrivals were published daily in newspapers across the country. Before they received the first phone call, relatives of Navy men often already knew that their sailor had arrived at a port along the West Coast.

The Army.., it's job complete.., it could go home.

Responsible for the massive undertaking of withdrawing an accumulation of a steady four year build up of forces, the Navy's "Operation Magic Carpet" quietly did the job. The convoluted "point system", having created more than a little apprehension as to when it would be possible to return to the States, made it seem probable Penn sailors would return by the Fall of 1946. Answering their letters and taking their calls, living up to his reputation, former Navy Lieutenant Jim Newpher, now a Penn Man himself, was busily taking applications from former Quaker Sailors. Anxious to get started, to get caught up, re-admission as quickly as possible was their top priority. After a few days "terminal leave", to begin making up for lost time.

Frequently processing Penn sailors through the Navy's suddenly quiet Philadelphia ship yard, rather than being discharged, BuPers was assigning certain of the returning officers to an "inactive duty" status. Before proceeding on home for a short "terminal leave", hopping the North bound Broad Street subway, and then the familiar West Philadelphia "42" car, a few chose to visit the Admissions office. Replying to their inquiries and heeding his invitation, they came to discuss their readmission application and to check on dorms, credits and course requirements. Surprised to be welcomed by former Navy Lieutenant Jim Newpher, they were pleased to hear that he had been newly appointed the University's Vice Dean of Admissions... And when he quickly advised them they could be slated to begin classes within a few weeks, they were more than satisfied that the side trip was well worth while.

Even though the noise, confusion , and uncertainty associated with the bustling anchorages of Eniwetok, Guam, Manila, Tokyo, Ulithi, Pavuvu, Yokohama, and Okinawa remained fresh in their minds... , by comparison, the busier and noisier West Philadelphia Campus appeared to be a quiet paradise.

CHAPTER IX.

"HOMEWARD BOUND"

"Fill up the mighty sparkling bowl
That I, a true and loyal soul
May drink and sing without controul,
To support my pleasure.
Thus may each jolly sailor live,
When fears and dangers o'er,
For past misfortunes never grieve,
When he's arriv'd on shore."
Sailors Drinking ditty....18th Century

With the "surrender" aboard the Missouri, and operations in Sagami Wan left behind to the daily arrival of increasingly numerous forces.. , U.S. Army and Marine Corps.. , the UDT received orders to head for Northern Honshu to complete a one Team operation.. , clearing the way for more troop landings.. Having totally disappeared, there would be no Jap opposition at Aomori Bay on Honshu's Northern tip. A Jap fishing and ship building village just South of the island of Hokkaido, it was as if it had been abandoned. Because of falsely spread rumors of American revenge, in fact the fearful inhabitants were hiding inside their wood and paper houses.

Completing the Aomori operation, the ship got underway for the West coast of Japan...; through the Tsugaru Strait between Honshu and Hokkaido, in the direction of Vladivostok, before turning South along the coast of Honshu in the Sea of Japan. With a "condition watch" set, the ship moved cautiously, as the gunners would periodically fire their twin 20 and 40 MMs at all floating mines of many origins. While the ship maneuvered to avoid the flotsam jetsam generated by years of aggressive U.S. Navy Submarine Warfare, at a point opposite Sado Island the helmsman was ordered to turn Eastward into a mine filled bay leading up a channel to the port city of Niigata.

Not wanting the Navy in that port city, the Japs did their best to discourage entry by sending out an old tug with a rather nondescript emissary to warn the U.S. ship off... . Dressed in parts of both an Army and a Naval uniform, the messenger turned out to be a disguised and hostile navy "harbor pilot". He warned of impending disaster, from anchored and floating mines, if the ship continued on the course set for that Sea of Japan port. Continuing in their attempt to thwart the U.S. Navy's landing operations, it was apparent that local Jap animosity had not been subdued. When the annoyed APD "skipper" finally ordered the Jap to have a minesweeper precede the U.S. ship and lead the way, he directed the helmsman to follow in the minesweeper's wake. The APD's Navigator carefully recorded "bearings" in marking the course on his chart for his future reference. Only a few short miles across the Sea of Japan, our inscrutable WWII Ally, China, led by it's flamboyant General Chiang Kai-shek, was finally free of it's Japanese nemesis after 14 years of persevering bloody resistance.

China was just over the horizon, the true domicile of the "setting" sun.. , indeed not the "rising" sun.. ! Recalling the few words that I knew from verse of Rudyard Kipling, the immortal British poet and writer of ballads.. , I repeated to myself... , over and over.. , those romantic words.. , "And the dawn comes up like thunder out of China 'cross the bay".

Returning again to Sagami Wan, the ship lay at anchor awaiting orders to the next operating area. While many UDTs remained aboard, the crew was kept busy running up salutes to the departing "heavy hitters"... , carriers and battlewagons of the Third Fleet. No desire to go ashore again in that smelly and repugnant land, it was time to make a "sea chest" out of damage control "shoring" lumber in the carpenter shop. Though many worked on their gear, a few UDTs continued to go ashore and to explore the now lightly occupied coastal towns.

Caught up on their sleep between "watches", there was suddenly an interest in the ship's little USO stocked library. And to play a little cribbage, and a lot of bridge.., often throughout the night in the ward room.

Finishing up the nightly bridge sessions, about 0400 the tantalizingly overpowering smell wafting from the galley told us that the bakers were about to take the ship's daily bread supply out of the big baking ovens.

Clandestinely, the "dummy's" mission was to go down the passageway, confiscate several hot crusty white loaves from the cooling racks just inside the galley hatch, liberate some butter from the galley, make certain of a full coffee pot.

Heretofore in short supply, and still being rationed in the States, butter had suddenly become plentiful. The ship's supply officer was besieged by Base and Fleet supply dumps at Guam, Ulithi and Eniwetok Atoll, as well as supply ships in the fleet train, who were doling out whatever a ship would agree to take. Perhaps a response to reports out of the USSR that American butter, rationed and carefully conserved in the U.S. for the war effort, was said to be in plentiful supply on Russian tables where it hadn't been seen in many years.

As the regular bridge game wound down, big chunks of hot crusty bread, spread thick with butter, were washed down with numerous mugs of hot fresh black coffee from the wardroom's coffee service. Having long before learned to accommodate, even appreciate, the crunch of the baked in weevils, that apparently were impossible to eliminate from wheat flour storage aboard U.S. Navy ships in the Pacific, UDTs devoured large quantities of the warm crunchy stuff. Weevils were simply accepted as a part of ship board life.., every ship had them.., the crews ate them.., the officers ate them.., and bread had never been more appetizing. It was one of those special Pacific war remembrances that Navy men would readily recall in the years to follow.

When Monday October the 8th came, and I began to realize that, although I had been doing it for three years or so, I was about to become lawfully eligible. Eligible that is…. to elbow my way up to the "City Hotel" bar, look "Murphy", the balding bartender straight in the eye, lay down my dime, and say, "one Flocks..,'Murph'.. , fill it to the rim and knock off the head".

Towards the end of chow that evening, while some UDTs were still chewing on their stringy, with fat and gristle, Australian mutton, the Teams grinning Steward's Mate walked quietly into the wardroom carrying a huge sheet cake flaming with candles… 21 of them… , to be precise. Baking the cake himself that afternoon, in green letters across the white icing, he had written "Happy Birthday" followed by my name. Taking the time to find out that my preference was moist, heavy, and chocolate…, it was so heavy that it sank to the bottom of our stomachs like a "runaway anchor". As far as anyone could remember, it was the only time that he had baked anything his entire time with the Team. Now when I recall that 1945 birthday in the place of that historic surrender, I am consciously sentimental of that long ago gesture. Franklin was neither a cook …or a baker. The wardroom was attended by APD Ward Room Stewards. Only recently I was surprised to learn that he had been seasick much of the time and stayed in his bunk.

Stewards Mate to the Team's twelve officers aboard the APD, Franklin took care of our laundry, kept our dress shoes shined, cleaned our quarters, kept us in fresh linens, made up our bunks, etc.. Granted a billet for a single Stewards Mate to join the Team's authorized complement, Franklin had been assigned to the Team after it had been commissioned and had not experienced the legendary UDT training and "hell week". Many of the junior officers were only 20 to 21 years when they were assigned a steward. With no Stewards in camp at the Fort Pierce "NCDU" Base, it was a total surprise when one day Franklin reported to the Team's tent camp on the side of Haleakala on Maui.

Necessarily a mobile outfit.. , on and off ships and landing craft.. , hopping from island to island.. , base to base.. , usually for just a short stint. But when it came to quarters, UDTs usually got the "short end of the stick". Others were given priority... , the crew when aboard ship and... , when ashore... , by a well ensconced "ship's company".

Conceivably, Franklin was subliminally associated with time spent at Penn. Where the famous 1740 founder's name, used on everything, was everywhere. And, though not delegated that responsibility, wherever we were, I made certain that he was fed... , and had adequate sleeping quarters. And that's as much as any of us got. The only "colored" sailor on the Team... , assigned to the "headquarters platoon", and not involved in the Team's operations... , he could find himself out of the activities taking place around him.

A gentle Mississippi farm boy with a wide smile, Franklin sported a drawl that, for those who did not know him, initially was almost impossible to understand. Although until the cake incident I had not been aware of it, he had apparently recognized the spontaneous concern for him. And had overheard Don Johnson mention the 8th of October date.

Sagami Wan was quiet and the days were dragging, daily news releases of returning ship's crews and troops celebrating in the U.S.A. titillated thoughts of home. Announced by BuPers several weeks earlier, the UDTs began to accept the fact that they better take seriously the "point system". Each day there were rumors of new, conflicting, and dispiriting revisions. Nevertheless, there were downward adjustments being made in the point requirements and... , since that increased the number of those eligible to return to the States... , there appeared to be a crack in the daylight of optimism.

Without notice, the Team's "CO", who unknown to any of us had apparently been negotiating to leave the Team, had received orders from BuPers to proceed to the States via Navy air... , a PBY. Lieutenant Commander J. Fletcher "Spike" Chace, over 30 and married with several kids, had a point advantage. Making him a civilian, BuPers placed him on inactive duty status, and some of us would receive his Christmas greeting from his home in New York City.

But for a 21 year old bachelor officer, with no dependents, the required initial points appeared to be discouragingly sufficient to keep him on active duty and in Japan for several more years.

At the musty bomb shattered former Japanese Yokosuka Naval Officer's Club, the popular drinking song in the fall of 1945 was sung to the tune of that sentimental wartime love song...., "Always";

I'll be overseas.. always..,
Standing "OOD's".. always...
(ref. "Officer of the Deck" watches)

When the things we've planned,
Need a helping hand,
I'll be in Japan.., Always.., Always...

When they count the score.., Always..,
I'll need two point's more.., Always..
(ref. , to the discharge point system)

Not for just for now..,
Not for just for then—
But I'll be in Japan.., Always....., Always......

And the most serious "scuttlebutt" concerned the surprise
Russian occupation of the Kurile Islands.., an ominous occurrence placing the future all the more in doubt.

The forward area Commander of UDTs opposed an inquiry
from BuPers concerning a proposal to reassign personnel to the
occupation forces in Japan or China... Charts were studied when
it was reported that four teams were to comb areas of China
looking for hidden POWs....., and to make a reconnaissance of the
Manchurian Russian border. When several UDTs made a quick
insertion into the recently Russian occupied Kuriles, charts of the
Sea of Japan and the coastline North of Vlalivostok became the
center of study. "Golden Gate in `48"... , began to take on meaning
again. Years passed before we would learn that Commander
Kauffman had dauntlessly fought the reassignment of UDTs. He
had successfully convinced BuPers that they had come to the
Pacific as a commissioned unit... , and would remain intact until
officially decommissioned back in the States. And Admiral Turner
backed him up.

Although there were still ships as far as you could see... , when
orders finally arrived, the number comprising the Third Fleet had
begun to steadily dwindle and thin out. As others weighed anchor,
hoisting their "homeward bound" pennants indicating that "Stateside", not China, was their destination, large gaps opened up in
the once crammed anchorage.

Ships about to shove off competed to "out do" each other when
hoisting their own many colored version of a "homeward bound"
pennant that trailed the length of over half of a ship.... , from the
top of the mast to beyond the stern.

Until the Fall of '45, wartime sailors had never seen the long
and colorful "Homeward Bound " pennants that implied another

reason for the traditional "happy ship". Suddenly these bright multi-colored "ship length" concoctions were everywhere.

Not to be surpassed, the APD crew went to work and constructed their version of an attention attracting long and colorful pennant that would rival that of a 45.000 ton battleship. With their special hand sewn "work of art" ready to be hoisted to the masthead, so were all hands ready to go.

Minutes after our sailing orders arrived, the Captain promptly went to the "squawk box" to pass the word. "Now hear this! Now hear this!... this is the Captain speaking"; there wasn't an officer or an enlisted man aboard not anticipating the enthusiastically awaited "Stateside" directive. Later rescinded, apparently as a result of the tragic sinking of the unescorted Heavy Cruiser Indianapolis, when only 316 of the crew of 1200 survived, earlier the Captain announced orders for the ship to sail alone for Pearl Harbor and the States via the "great circle"... , the Northern route. The same Northern route followed by Yamamoto's Fleet in early December 1941... this time APD "Young" would approach Pearl from the North.

When the APD entered "Pearl" on October 25.... Navy Day... , 1945..., the ship was given the traditional salute by an imposing array of combat ships of the Third and Fifth Fleet at dock side or at anchor. All "decked out" for the first peace time Navy Day since 1941, strings of pennants ran fore and aft from each ship; each with it's own colorful version of a "homeward bound" pennant fluttering from the top of the masthead. Right in the heart of it's greatest defeat, of it's then 170 year history, four years later the Navy was putting on one hell of a party.

Anchored off shore, the ships "LCPRs" were kept busy taking alternating port and starboard liberty parties ashore. For me, an afternoon ashore for a couple of quiet scotches at an unusually subdued Pearl Harbor Officer's Club filled with guys whose main agenda was to be home for Christmas. Now that the war was behind us, apparently the base was loaded with previously hoarded supplies and all types of gear stored for use in "Operation Olympic". . Anxious to peddle it to whatever ship was coming through... , no matter which direction she was taking, the supply officer brought on board a large quantity of cigarettes permitting anyone to purchase whatever they wanted at 5 cents a pack. Most Navy men smoked in that period and great quantities of all brands were sold.

After almost a month without a "mail call", the Fleet Post Office, short stopping the mail weeks before, sent a mail boat filled with bags of welcome news from the States.

A batch of letters from "S.B.", having graduated in June from WHS before spending the Summer as a lifeguard at Eagles Mere, wrote excitedly of her life at school in Englewood, New Jersey and her weekend trips into New York. Her plans were to be in "Billtown" over Christmas... and, "now that the war is over.., will you be home to spend some time over the holidays? If you can't make it, we can meet later in New York." Though all hands were ready and anxious to move out... , it was November 1st and we were half way around the world from Pennsylvania and New Jersey; a much bigger world in 1945. The frequent announcements in the progression of the "point system" did not provide any semblance of an illusion that any of us would be home for Christmas. I wrote back, "it will probably have to be New York."

Anticipating a reassignment to one of the "magic carpet" ships of the Pacific Fleet, before returning to sea, California would only be a temporary respite. Nevertheless, when conversations turned to the only topic that was popular, visions of a white Christmas in Pennsylvania were kept alive. UDTs were a little optimistic.

All of a sudden a proliferation of fresh tattoos began to appear on the shoulders, arms, and chests of UDTs returning from Honolulu. Evidence, when we finally pulled out of Pearl... , that would give those UDTs something to remember Navy Day 1945 for a lifetime. The most popular tattoo, and one that made me think seriously..., a colorful "clipper ship", backed by a bright orange setting sun, captioned "Homeward Bound" in a half circle over the top of the masts.

Even today, I half regret that I did not have that one etched on the upper arm. After no contact for almost a half century, a few years ago I had lunch on a warm day in Philadelphia with a UDT from my platoon. Wearing a short sleeve shirt, the tattoos, for which he had been remembered, had become faded and indistinguishable... merely faded blue blotches on his forearms.

The days passed slowly. At home the early chill of Winter had already colored the leaves of the forests along the "Endless Mountains". And with a full complement aboard, the ship seemed more crowded as it lay at anchor off Ford Island. Edging further into November, with concern for the much discussed "leave" and expense of a trip to the East coast, UDTs began to pass up liberty to stay on board to conserve the family treasury. Should "leave" be granted with orders to report to a station or ship on the West Coast, it would be necessary to return to California. That could deplete a major part of a sailor's net worth and spell "fiscal crisis" for most UDTs.

Before daylight on the 9th of November, after the dock handlers finally cast off the lines, the Captain smartly backed the ship away from the pier without the help of tugs or the rest of the Navy. When the ship rounded "Diamond Head", and the bow again pointed toward the East, the UDTs relaxed a trifle more confident

that this time they were truly "Homeward Bound". At least a..,
"California here we come.. right back where we started from".

Soon to be just a memory, private thoughts became whimsical
when the UDTs began to contemplate the reality of missing those
all night bridge games and the early morning hot buttered crusty
weevil bread... . Lifetime recollections of those tropical nights
lying on a wet steel deck up forward, while hanging over the side
to watch the ship's bow slice the brightly illuminated phosphores-
cent warm Pacific, were never to be repeated for most. It certainly
has not been my good fortune to relive those enduring experiences. They would miss seeing the extravaganza of "flying fish" as
they scattered in the ship's wake and, because of the low "free-
board" of an APD hull, flop momentarily on the forward deck
before maneuvering back into the water rushing past the bow.

Ordering all engines reduced to 1/3 ahead, on the "final 1000
yards" of the return from Sagami Wan, the Captain, a cerebral
Harvard man, brought the little weathered APD swiftly across
San Diego Harbor. Evidently concluding that he would have one
last little celebration of his own, the ship moved deliberately on
a swift straight course toward a position along side of a very short
pier. Beginning to look as though the ship would end up in the
hills of San Diego along side the now highly publicized City Zoo,
the Commander was putting on a pretty impressive performance
for the UDT Staff, as well as for the Navy band and Red Cross
ladies waiting on the dock. Having taken control of the bridge,
and the tricky maneuver of unassisted docking, he snapped sharp
orders to the helm and to the engine room...., "back'er down".... .
The taut little rusty and salt weathered ship shuddered from
stem to stern as the deck crew fought to keep their footing while
preparing to lower the fenders and take aboard the mooring lines
from the handlers on the dock. With the ship tied down in a matter
of minutes, the crew and the UDTs crowded the rails while their
attention and speculation was diverted by the presence of the
attractive Red Cross Ladies. The Navy Band on the dock "struck
up" it's own version of some of the popular tunes of 1945-, among
them two UDT favorites, "Sentimental Journey" and "Atchinson
Topeka and the Santa Fe". And old sailors will "square" their hats
and straighten up a bit when "Anchors Aweigh" recalls youthful
marching days at "boot camp", the Academy, or Midshipman
School. Wasting no time, the crew lowered the gangway and
cleared the deck to bring aboard the welcoming party.

Only a few hours earlier, as the sun came up out of the wide
ground swells of the Pacific, and the APD closed to about one
hundred miles off the coast, the UDTs executed orders to jettison
tons of explosives. Instructed by the officer on watch to cut the
engines to "ahead one-third", the ship slowed to permit the

unhappy chore of emptying the "hold" of it's hoard of tetrytol, TNT, explosive filled rubber hose, C-2 plastic explosive, bangalores, prima cord, caps, fuse, and 55 lb charges. With the wide deck hatch opened, the UDTs formed several "bucket brigade" type lines to pass the explosive to the rail where the last man gave it a heave over the side and away from the hull. With additional space under the hatch, the Team began to assemble their gear under the boom in preparation to lowering it over the side to waiting trucks on the pier. To comply with custom inspection regulations, Officer's made a passing cursory inspection of enlisted gear and authorized their own by signature. With the gang plank lowered, and a "gangway" watch set on the pier and on the deck, the Red Cross ladies were the first to aboard. Leaning over the side for the best view, the crew mustered a resounding cheer as they made their way up the gang plank. Followed by "white hats" carrying crates of bottled fresh milk and boxes with what turned out to be home made pies, cookies, and cakes... , the sailors who got the most acclaim that day... , were three Petty Officers from the Fleet Post Office.

With several large urns of coffee set out on deck by the stewards, all hands took time out for an hour of coffee, fresh milk and pastry...; and especially the chit chat with the gray uniformed ladies of the Red Cross. Still standing in formation on the dock, the Navy Band had kept right on with their spirited medley of popular war tunes until finally joining the crew and UDTs for the refreshments up on the U.S.S. Walter X. Young's deck.

California's brown hills never looked so good... , or smelled so fresh and clean!

PHOTOGRAPHS

"Professional soldiers are sentimental men, for all the harsh realities of
their calling. In their wallets and in their memories they carry bits of
philosophy, fragments of poetry, quotations from the Scriptures, which,
in times of stress and danger speak to them with great meaning".
General Mathew B. Ridgeway, USA:
"My Battles in War and Peace", January 1956

Recollections of the typical WWII sailor would seem to substantiate
General Ridgeway's personal memoirs. And acknowledge that wallets
had been overflowing with photos, poetic notes, prayers, memorable
clippings . . ., in a sort of capsulated album. And, beginning with those
well traveled wallets harboring deeply private sentiments, those who
were drawn in to such a dedicated avocation, only for the war years,
inevitably carry that experience a degree or two deeper than any other
in life.

Recognizing early on that their wartime encounters would be relatively short lived . . ., never to be repeated . . ., American Sailors returned
to civilian life with troves of clippings, USO and Red Cross mementoes,
citations, menus, photos, "V-Mail" letters, medals, sets of "orders",
flags, and guns . . . . . . Found cluttering the walls of dens and offices in
the most remote hamlets, and cherished increasingly by old sailors, are
photographs of then young shipmates, old fighting ships, and their old
"outfits", "companies" and "battalions" on parade.

An old Japanese proverb reads,
"Among flowers, the best is the cherry blossom; among men, the best is
the soldier."

While the Americans filled their albums recording historic events,
posturing for tourist attractions, shooting amusing "mug shots" and
scenery . . . ., all types of casual incidents, a minuscule incite into the
enemies passion and interest in this type of memento appears to have
been mainly more formal photographs reflecting life in the military.

The following pages include photographs, articles, and cartoons
selected from an album assembled almost a half century ago, in the late
1940's.

And as always, as required by U.S. Navy regulations, none of the
opinions or assertions in "Quaker Sailors" reflect those of the U.S. Navy.

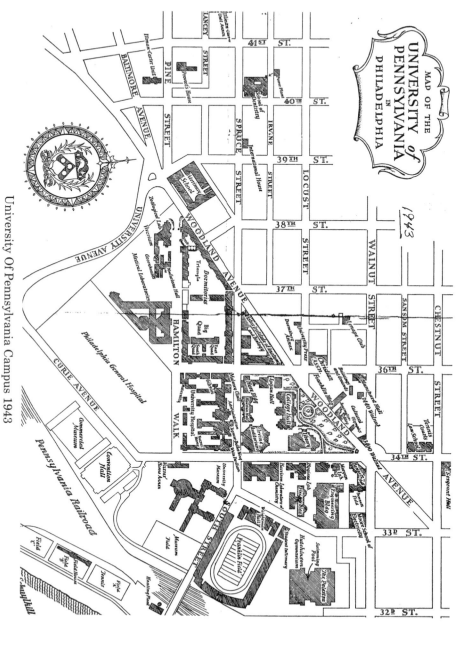

University Of Pennsylvania Campus 1943

Outdoor USO Plaza; Opposite Broad St. Station

"Walls of Ivy .... E.F. Smith # 20"
L. to .R.: F.A. Halkett, Author, F.R. Hammerschmidt

"2nd Platoon: Coming (us) and Going (them) !"

"At Balikpapan: Just what Betsy (Ross) ordered!"

"Smokey Joe ma-day doan-o-koo-ra-ee DESS-ka ?"
(College Hall trans. "How Far Is Smokey Joes ?"

"Admiral Yamamamto Directed the
Pearl Harbor Attack from Battleship Nagato"

"Not Exactly 'Navy Blue and Gold !"

"HMS King George: A Royal Neighbor"

"The Last day for Australian Mutton"
L. to R.: McDonnell, "Maud", Roberts, the Author

"Kaetens scuttled at Yokosuka"

"A Wharton Entrepreneur in Yokosuka ?"

"Just the Way Mike D. Described It"

"General Douglas MacArthur at His Imperial Hotel H.Q."

"*My dear!   Not only did he survive all the campaigns in the South Pacific—he made it all the way across the U. S. at Christmas!*"

"Christmas 1945: What Happened to 'Golden Gate in '48 ?'"

"If you have a daughter, Sir! Set her on your knee.
But if you have a son..., send the bastard out to sea!"

"The Battalion on Parade 1943"

CHAPTER X.

"Homeward Bound.... From Sea To Shining Sea"

The friend described the Japanese as, "trying to rewrite history.
Instead of teaching young people about the events of World War II
in the Pacific, they were trying to avoid the issue or recast it completely.
"There are many living with the scars that refute those altered history
books, But when they die, who will refute the books then?"

Located off the mainland from San Diego, the Amphib Base on
Coronado Island would later be designated the new home to the
UDTs. The original NCDU camp at Fort Pierce, as well as the
secret advanced base on the leeward side of Maui's Haleakala,
had already been relegated to suffer the consequences of having
out lived their wartime usefulness. Coronado, with it's beautiful
Southern California climate and cold Pacific surf, remains the
West coast base to accommodate the secret world wide missions
involving ... UDTs... , and their successors... Navy SEALS.. , for
the last half century.

Accustomed to moving in and out of bases... , on and off ships...,
the UDTs settled comfortably into the best quarters ever experienced since initially reporting to a camp of temporary tents in
Fort Pierce, Florida. These were solid two story BOQs... , only two
bunks and four officers to a room... , windows to let in fresh air...,
lockers big enough to hang uniforms... , a "head" and shower with
plenty of hot water on every deck.. , fresh linens... , and with
"NAVY" imprinted in big blue letters, thick white wool blankets.
Only a half mile to the "Mess"... , the cafeteria type operation
served real beef hamburgers that weren't half filled with bread
crumbs. And never served Australian mutton! A little taste of the
"peace time" Navy... , and literally living in the lap of luxury.

Surprised to discover that the BOQ was maintained by German
POWs... , UDTs were dumbfounded to find the prisoners were
permitted to wander in and out of their quarters at will. Accustomed to keeping their weapons with them in the BOQ, the UDTs
became a little cautious.

After making certain their gear made it from the pier to the
BOQ, as always, the immediate destination for many was a phone
booth... , a call home. After that.., to go ashore.., get away from the
base... , and the Navy... , for a few hours in Coronado. Ashore with

regular people in civilian surroundings, to enjoy a greasy hamburger and onion, that hadn't been supplemented with a lot of bread crumbs. And a thick chocolate shake made with creamy stateside ice cream. For the lucky few, wives and fiancees would be arriving by train and plane within days. One returning much enraptured UDT Ensign, expecting to have his young fiancee rush out to the coast from Florida, learned for the first time that she had capriciously become engaged, a second time. And to another UDT. Instead of meeting him, as her letters had led him to expect, she would come to California to meet her new "intended", a UDT that she met after the jilted fiance had already "shipped out" to the Pacific. Her new fiance, having only recently wound up at Fort Pierce at about the time that the war ended, and with Maui training cancelled, waited at Coronado.

To their ever growing list of "liberty towns", the UDTs were about to add another port.. , San Diego.. . Having listened to the recounted scuttlebutt surrounding the nearby Del Coronado Hotel... , officers donned their best available uniforms to "recon" that beautiful nearby historic landmark. Although most Southern California evenings turn comfortably cool in the Winter, very few returning UDTs had "dress blues" available on the West coast.

And Navy Men brought some of the most comely and dignified young ladies in Southern California to those balmy Del Coronado homecoming nights. Although the tally was building each evening, the Southern California belles found themselves far out numbered by even greater numbers of returning Navy men. As Navy ships and crews, as well as the personnel of the other forces, were funneled through the old port from the forward areas, the Del Coronado management lavished them with it's hospitality. And played nightly host to a continual homecoming party of officers returning daily from all areas of the Pacific. Playing every night on the manicured hotel lawn, a "big band" provided music for dancing on the wide lantern lit verandas. Lounging around relaxing in the bar, on the porches, and on the lawn, sailors could test the waters and retell their own versions of the Pacific War. And were looking to experience the same camaraderie they had known in the flimsy officer clubs on the various islands and bases as they crossed and recrossed the Pacific all the way to Yokosuka. Only a few UDTs would over extend themselves when they promptly discovered the price of a "scotch" at the Del Coronado was a lot "stiffer" than that purchased with "chits' at clubs on remote islands of the Pacific. Scattered in groups across the porches and lawn, UDT sailors joined with the band, as they had done all across the Pacific, to sing the nostalgic war tunes as well as the songs of their Alma Mater; particularly those forever haunting sentimental and meaningful tunes of World War II... , "Bell Bottom Trousers", "Remember Pearl Harbor", "Don't Sit Under the Apple Tree", "White Cliffs of Dover", "Here Comes the Navy", "Lili Marlene", "Anchors Aweigh".. , and even the special UDT ditty, "Out in Front of the Navy". More than just a little sentimental, it permitted lasting memories of many happy Navy times at the famous old hotel. And for many of those young sailors, those Del Coronado nights have long been remembered as kind of a last farewell to their youth.

With many of the team occupied entertaining wives or fiancees, two nights before Thanksgiving I boarded the ferry alone intending to explore San Diego. A much smaller village in 1945, the "downtown" retained the flavor of a typical "turn of the century" waterfront sailor town. Though it had it's "honky tonk" bars, tattoo parlors, Army-Navy stores, uniform shops, "ship's stores" and warehouses, it was not a West Coast Norfolk. Unlike Norfolk... , it was clean.. , quiet... , and orderly... , and a pretty good liberty town in 1945.

Having a nose for finding a rough and tumble sailor's bar, and attracted by the colorful outside facade depicting a cave with pirates and pulchritudinous ladies, led me to a garish and noisy "Pirate's Den". Just the kind of bar that the UDTs had discovered from West Palm Beach... , to Market Street in San Francisco... , and to the "run down" shanties of downtown Honolulu, where past recorded "liberties" were recalled over and over. And the "Pirate's Den" was a "ladies sorority" as compared with the infamous "Krazy Kat" in downtown Norfolk. Nevertheless.. , it was soon evident that the "Den" would live up to it's descriptive mural and it's big sign on the outside wall, "Girls, Girls, Girls". Minutes after being seated near the stage, which was at the same level with the customer's tables, there was barely time to order a bottle of "Hamms" beer before first the lights blinked and were then lowered as the band erupted with a fanfare. Signaling that the show was about to begin, the five piece combo began with a medley of popular "show tunes" just as a small chorus line of voluptuous young ladies made their entrance from the side of the stage. Under bright lights, and scantly attired, there was little doubt that the "Pirate's Den" owner had assembled a seductively endowed line of talented chorus girls to perform on his stage. Tall, with freckles and long red hair, one especially familiar face was readily dismissed as being too improbable. The young lady, of whom I seemed to be reminded, lived in West Philadelphia, attended West Catholic High, was brought up in a sheltered and strict religious home environment, and most certainly was in a women's college somewhere. The "Pirate's Den" would be the last place to look for her!

Yet, when her eyes kept periodically locking on mine for a fleeting second, there appeared to be an uncertainty of recognition.

As the band continued their noisy "show tune" music, and the chorus line legged their way through a peppy routine, the enthusiastic mostly Navy audience overcame the bedlam in the low ceiling room with their own loud conversations . But, with long shapely legs and full busts bursting out of their costumes, the chorus line had no trouble retaining the sailor's complete attention. When the lights were gradually lowered, changing their pace... , the combo and the gals broke into, "Spring is Busting Out All Over"... , a "catchy" light and happy tune from "Oklahoma". About the third chorus, when the words "busting out all over" reached a crescendo, a drum roll drowned out the other instruments of the band. And one of the especially well endowed young dancers burst out of what must have been an exhausted "bra". All conversations were supplanted by the sudden suspension of lower jaws as her endowments and charms overflowed into the faces of the audience.

Caught off guard, the sailors were certain it was a fortunate stroke of good luck to be in attendance that night. The initial shock... , followed by stunned silence.. , followed by smug suspicion. But when the girls began to run off the side of the stage, spontaneous applause, followed by standing rousing cheers, brought them running back on stage to acknowledge the audience's enthusiasm. Just about the right dose that would keep most sailors in their seats drinking for another hour or two through several performances. Still uncertain whether the last incident was a part of the chorus's routine, deciding to not hang around to find out.., I started for the door. Somehow I was not surprised to hear my name as I passed through the inner foyer to make my exit. Without even turning, I recognized the voice of Pat Flynn from Philadelphia. Having met on the Penn Campus almost three years earlier, she had been a pretty red headed senior at Philadelphia's West Catholic. Proof that it was a much smaller country in December 1945.

Though tired, and intent on returning to the BOQ, since she would get off after the next show, we agreed to meet about an hour and fifteen minutes later. Walking back to the Pirates Den after about an hour, I found her waiting outside. Sharing an apartment only a few blocks from the "Den" with another chorus member, both could conveniently walk to work. Walking through the dark deserted San Diego streets to her apartment, we talked about the last several years since leaving "Philly" and caught up as much as she wanted to. How she traveled across country with her roommate, barely enough money, and no plans. With an exceptional face and long red hair, in Philadelphia she had been employed as a model while still in high school and immediately upon graduation. About to graduate, she had given me a large colored portrait from her model's portfolio. Regretfully, it could not fit into my "seabag" and, before shipping out to Midshipman school, entrusting it to a roommate, left it on the mantle over the fireplace in suite 20 of "Edgar Fahs Smith".

After three years, she had become even more beautiful than when she had been a model in "Philly". A little fuller in the face and all the strategic places, she was no longer "string bean" thin. And probably less employable as a model. Finding it difficult to save enough money to cover the train fare, she had all but given up returning to her parents Philadelphia home in time for Christmas. With rapidly growing unemployment due to the "cut back" in war work, competition was stiff in this part of Southern California. Singing and dancing in the Pirates Den chorus was the most lucrative work that she could find. As nice as ever, understandably the "Pirate's Den" management was delighted to have her in their chorus.

We renewed our West Philadelphia friendship whenever I was able to get into San Diego and, on a number of occasions, when she came over to Coronado. Increasingly also anxious to be home for the holidays, she borrowed the funds to cover the train fare. And wired of her arrival in Philadelphia and that she would be at her parents home over the holidays.

Along with all of the UDT gear, I had been storing seven disassembled Jap rifles in my "sea chest". Picked up in the islands, they were brought ashore to Coronado in several seabags. Concluding that it was time to find out what they would bring in the souvenir market, I placed a notice on the base bulletin board. And promptly sold them... , all in one day... , for twenty five dollars each. Although they were a sad excuse for a rifle, Navy men going in both directions bought them for souvenirs. Just returning from the Pacific, some of my customers were happy to have a last chance to acquire a "war souvenir". Others, heading in the opposite direction, fearing that they wouldn't be available later, sent them home before even leaving the states.

And from a "captured", beat up, barely floating enemy Destroyer, I had managed to acquire a Jap sextant with Nazi markings manufactured in Germany. Unlike today, when Japanese have become known for their leadership in technical manufacturing, apparently they did not have the knowledge or expertise to make their own equipment of that type. It appeared they were also dependent upon the Germans for optical items such as good binoculars. Attempting to sell that sextant for over a month, I received help when, one night at the Del Coronado, Draper

Kauffman suggested that I take it to an acquaintance of his who operated a Navigation School on the San Diego waterfront. When the proprietor agreed to buy it for a hundred dollars cash, I promptly accepted. Although not satisfied with the price, it was my only offer and I was running out of time. Concerned with the impending railroad trip to the East coast, it was preparation for traveling light.

Complete with it's own very heavy and elaborately sturdy wooden case, that German sextant was a beautiful piece. Destined to become a collector's item, I have often regretted that I did not keep it.

All of my other weapons and gear, Japanese and Navy issue, had been sent home in seabags over a period of several weeks by way of Railway Express.

Needing a few "gag" gifts for a "last liberty" party with several UDTs with orders to report to their home Naval Districts, at a downtown department store I was assisted by a personable and attractive eighteen year old San Diego Naval Officer's daughter. All Navy, and very familiar with the Del Coronado, accepting an invitation, she proved to be a lot of fun. Agreeing to assist in picking out the gifts, our choices appeared to coincide. Unflappable, she could happily chat on about anything. And did!

As Christmas approached, anticipating orders to "ship out", I knew my "coast" days were dwindling. Still, obtaining action on "leave" orders continued to be stymied. Planning to remain on the East coast, and return to classes the following Fall, unless reassigned by the Navy, the possibility of returning to California in 1945, or the foreseeable future, seemed to be tenuous. And, as it turned out, did not return for over twenty three years.

With a lot of pride, Annette Stuart would relate, what had been a great love story...., her parents war time romance and marriage. Her father, by 1945 a Navy Commissioned Warrant Officer, had met, fallen in love, and married her mother 27 years earlier, while serving as a young enlisted man in France during World War I..., in 1918.... A warm and attractive couple.., she having retained a very distinct French accent, he typical of a career "mustang", both went out of their way to be very hospitable to a 21 year old Navy man.

While our lives were swept along, and regularly changed direction in that immediate post war period, our increasingly infrequent correspondence continued for a number of years. Meeting.., leaving..., moving on..., and never returning had become a way of life for many WWII GIs.

Although, with each passing day the war was left further behind, the "point system" continued to cast it's ominous, "I'll believe it when I see it", shadow.

As BuPers proceeded to methodically issue orders, at the same time resolving to prevent "logjams" in the processing centers, UDTs went about their business. With fewer people to keep things together, tied down with "ComPhibsTraPacAdmins UDT until finally released a few days before Christmas, our "shore time" had been curtailed.

Somewhere.. , someone.. , at BuPers had been reminded that every UDT had responded to a call for "volunteers". And, in deference to the secret "extra hazardous duty"... , the Navy Department... , BuPers... , issued an "AlNav" authorizing the Commander of Underwater Demolition Teams... , Amphibious Forces... , Pacific Fleet... , at Coronado... , to recommend eligible UDTs to select their choice of duty.

Making a pitch to recruit for the post war UDTs... , to "ship over" with a "regular Navy" rate or commission... , as always, Commander Draper Kauffman was very persuasive. When news had not reached Coronado, that the dusty camp of tents on the side of Mount Haleakala over looking the Kealikahiki Channel and Maalaea Bay had already been torn down, those volunteering to remain with the UDTs had visions of returning to a leisurely life of "sun and surf" on the beaches of Maui. And Kauffman's effusive scenario did nothing to discourage that conjecture.

With no options offered, my initial and only request was for a billet as an Athletic Officer at a V-12 college. BuPers's response was immediate... , V-12 Units had been instructed to phase out their programs and to complete the decommissioning of their commands.

Not certain as to what to request, UDTs only knew they did not want to start over with a ship's crew. Not ordinary sailors, UDTs did not see themselves at sea again on some endless "magic carpet" assignment returning GIs to the West Coast from hundreds of different ports and bases in the Western Pacific. Appropriately named "magic carpet", the hastily contrived Navy ferry service was created to bring service personnel back to the States at "flank speed".

The "ALNAV" also provided for UDTs to request a choice of duty location. Requesting a shore billet, and specifically the East Coast..., my request stated the "Northeast".

A "beach" assignment in the Shore Patrol, the duty requested in my second application, seemed to have been already spelled out. Volunteering for duty in the Navy, one never had to take a chance on random assignments doled out by BuPers. Orders from Washington were returned within a few days... .

Having already been received by the "C.O." of the new UDT Training Command, BuPers's orders provided for a few days leave before reporting to "S P" headquarters at the Navy Department. In an unusual twist.. , a first for me.. , separate orders specified quarters at the BOQ 2 at the Naval Gun Factory. Release from assignment with COMPHIBSTRAPACADMINS UDT STAFF was to be at their convenience.

Any enthusiasm for the new assignment was promptly over-shadowed by an increasingly apprehensive first priority... , finding a timely way to get to the East Coast and still have some leave time. With transportation already taxed to the limit, newspapers ran daily stories of returning G.I.s waiting for days in Los Angeles and San Francisco railroad stations for space to Chicago. If you could get as far as the "Windy City"... , train service was reported good the rest of the way to the East Coast.

Travelers, mostly GIs in December 1945, from Chicago to the "main line" of the East Coast rail corridor, were being jammed into crowded coaches. Calling up all of their available equipment to work around the clock, the Pennsylvania's answer was special trains. When others were taking off to enjoy the holidays for the first time in four or five years, train crews were putting in long hours for weeks at a time. With old coaches packed to "standing room only", Pennsy's passengers were squeezed aboard a train even if the GIs had to stand the entire distance. And no complaints!

When their orders arrived at Coronado, wasting no time, UDTs were on their way East. A few, disregarding a muster that could record their absence, took off immediately. Missing? A little discipline! In the malaise of teams being hastily decommissioned, the confusion of personnel rapidly being ushered out of the Navy, bases being dismantled around them by men still stationed there, and growing rows of ships without crews were being tied up in reserve anchorages at a rate that resulted in many not being "mothballed" for years. Attached to the UDT Staff, all I needed was a replacement.

Having been the recipient of many German prisoners from the North African Campaign, the POWs literally had the run of the Coronado base. They cleaned and made beds in the BOQ, were janitors for the buildings, and maintained the considerable California landscaping on the grounds. They were everywhere.. , unsmiling, but working, in very pleasant conditions and sunny weather. Notwithstanding, their large numbers, and status as POWs, brought a continuous set of problems to be disentangled by those standing "watch". With fewer people, and "watch" schedules posted weeks in advance, there appeared little chance of convincing the "Exec" to cut my orders until a replacement came in with a returning team.

Home for Christmas in 1946.. , not 1945.. , seemed a more likely expectation. Not all those assigned to base staff were as concerned and, using a little UDT "sneak and peek", "borrowed" the Yeoman's "C. O." stamp to endorse their own orders. Leaving those remaining behind to find replacements to stand their duty, those with orders in hand could take off. Figuring the war was over... , they did!

With departure dates finally approved, and orders endorsed, Don Johnson, from Detroit, and I were already geared and ready to take off for Los Angeles. Forewarned, it was a sure thing that we would wait in Union station a few days before finding space aboard a passenger coach for Chicago.

Having sent winter uniforms home a year earlier, and other gear in recent weeks, we were set to travel light. With only light weight khakis available for the trip East, before he took off, I remembered to borrow a "foul weather" jacket from Axel Brax, a UDT from Smolen, Kansas. Slowing down for deep snow, and a frigid wintry ride along the Northern rail route to Chicago, the jacket, which I promptly mailed to Brax's home in Kansas, had served very usefully.

Departing Coronado and San Diego in the early morning, still dark when arriving at Los Angeles, the terminal was crowded with sprawled and dozing GIs waiting for the next train East.. . Any train.. , just to get moving in the right direction. Entering the terminal on the run, the loudspeaker announced the departure of an already made up "special" leaving for Chicago within the hour, "Those holding tickets may board immediately... , all a board!!"

With ticket window lines backed up, those having already paid their fare were hurriedly passed through the gate permitting them to find a seat on the waiting string of what turned out to be ancient passenger cars. Local newspapers, picked up later along the route, reported that the "special" was the early result of the railroad's answer to the much broadcast West Coast "bottleneck". Supplementing their regular schedules, most of the country's railroads had ordered the operation of "specials" through the end of December.

Earlier that week, although doubtful they would be used before the first of the year... , Johnson and I had purchased tickets as far as the "Windy City".

With passenger space for those heading East critically short for weeks, only a few days before Christmas the train situation became increasingly bleak. Thousands of returning GIs, all attempting to cross the country in late December.... , were determined to make it home in time for the holidays. A one time event.., railroads all over the country were making an all out effort to cope with it. Yet cartoons, editorials, jokes, and newspaper "headlines", disparaging their efforts, would clamorously deplore the situation.

Illustrating two grandiloquent matriarchs gazing at a photograph of a Marine, in one cartoon, the "leatherneck's" mother remarked, "My dear! Not only did he survive all of the campaigns in the South Pacific.. , he made it all the way across the U.S. at Christmas!"

Frequently, those GIs attempting to get across country had been out of the States for a long time. Some had not had a Christmas at home for as long as four or five years. Listening to a record of "Bing" crooning "White Christmas", while sitting around in some gloomy barracks or on a ship, wasn't going to do it.. ! Not the Christmas of 1945.

When the "address system" repeated the "boarding" announcement on that chilly morning a few days before Christmas, most of the GIs in the "LA" Terminal had been sitting or stretched out for days waiting, in various states of repose, to hear those welcome words, "all aboard"! A few were even caught sleeping. Leaving long before dawn, having "thumbed it" most of the way along the coast highway, Johnson and I walked and ran the last mile. Entering the station at a full stride, we followed right behind the wrought iron gates as they swung wide. And followed on the heels of a conductor who pointed the way. Heeding his pointed finger, we headed straight for a string of old coaches and boarded through the first opened door.

Expecting to do a lot better than the first stripped down and worn coaches, we moved through some pretty sad looking cars until we found one that seemed to be "as good as it got". Tossing our "seabags" up on the baggage rack over two of the less abused seats, we proceeded to insure they were physically occupied until the train got underway. Making certain not to leave at the same time, we held on to and defended those two worn seats for the next four days. Any short term occupant, in either of our few absences, understood that it was just that.

Although a canteen had been set up in the middle of the train in what normally would have been the mail car, there would be only a few trips for food. And on trips to the "head", one of us always remain to "hold the fort". No one complained when all of the old coaches were filled beyond capacity, not even those who had to do the standing. Darkened at night, when GIs in the seats would begin to doze, those standing would lay down in the aisles. A few even managed to stretch out up on the baggage racks.

Whatever had to be endured was over shadowed by the expectation of arriving home for the holidays. Although a far less possibility for those traveling further East, those in the area surrounding Chicago would certainly spend Christmas at home... And there were ominous rumors of a lapse in train connections out of Chicago, where two stations served as "hubs" for numerous trains to the cities of the Mid-West as well as the East.. . Confusion and delays were attributed to uncertain train schedules, as well as unsatisfactory connections between the two stations. Once again, with backed up passenger traffic the culprit, the arrival of those heading for the East coast cities appeared to be increasingly doubtful. Held on "side tracks" several times to allow express "troop trains" to pass , our "special", winding it's way through the mountains and across the plains, made only five stops along the entire route before reaching Illinois.

Already packed with GIs exclusively bound for the "Windy City", additional passengers were rarely permitted aboard. Whenever the train made one of it's infrequent stops, the GIs poured off to buy whatever food that was available. Operating news stands in many stations, the American News Company quickly sold out of whatever newspapers were on hand. Read cover to cover by the GIs, and "dog-eared" within hours, their entire substantial weekly issues of Life magazines were snapped up in minutes. Hoping to find improving news of the Chicago confusion, the "homeward bound" GIs lined up to buy a five cent local newspaper, all the time with their fingers crossed that the latest accounts would indicate the Chicago "bottleneck" would be broken before they switched trains.

Back at Coronado, UDTs had observed first hand a spontaneous and brisk business initiated in private transportation from San Diego and Los Angeles to the Mid-West... , to Kansas City or St. Louis. "Wildcat" drivers offered to take a car full of sailors to Kansas City for one hundred dollars per man.., a little more to St. Louis. Although the Navy posted warnings of exploitation, those believing their situation to be desperate were ready to "cut" whatever deal was necessary. The condition of the cars, as well as the drivers, made the UDTs dubious. With an accumulation of "back pay" in their pockets, all they asked was for the driver to keep his word and get them to Kansas City or to St. Louis. With no concept as to what they would find upon arrival at those two cities, but with no information to the contrary, sailors were confident they would find a way to get home..... .

Stories of GIs, beating them up, and taking back their money upon arriving at their destination, were reported by returning drivers. As the time grew short, increasing numbers of sailors, deciding it was their last opportunity to get home by the 25th, were determined to take a chance. And they couldn't match the convenience... , to walk a few feet outside the Coronado base gate, and have a car waiting to take them to Kansas City.

Jammed with those "homeward bound" from the Pacific, as the darkened train's progress slowed down through the snowy mountain passes, and made it's way across the great plains, the long held tension of it's passengers gradually succumbed to the relaxing assurance of a country abruptly at peace for the first time in four years. As with others on board, Johnson and I would partially doze while reflecting on the unexpected consequences of our good fortune. What we had been expecting to be doing at that very time half way around the world in cold rough water, off heavily defended rocky shores of Kyushu, was to clear a "beach head" for the most ambitious amphibious assault ever undertaken. The logistics involved in keeping the United States Fleet at sea, and pulling off that operation, is mind boggling even today. Unlike prior Pacific campaigns, the Navy had been preparing for Northern cold weather and to cope with wintry storms at sea. And even more incomprehensible, an amphibious beach landing operation in the cold and rough early winter surf. If the loss of ships and men sustained in the Okinawa Operation were to be comparable for "Operation Olympic", in relation to the size of the forces involved, and there was no reason to believe that they would not, there would be massive losses of both. Losses attributed to exposure to the weather and the freezing water could contribute to the Navy's dilemma.

Four days and four nights! Johnson and I patiently endured what is now remembered as a very bitter early Winter.. , and the rigors of a cold ride in archaic coaches. It was as though.. , mutually we were still dubious as to where we had been and where we were going. All military, and having disembarked from ships and transports only days earlier... , those on board had only been in the States for a matter of hours before passing through LA's Union Station.

Others on that Chicago special, their own "outfits" also destined to attack Kyushu in late October.. , early November... , watched in disbelief to see that all change with a couple of bombs. And seemed so infeasible that we would awaken to find ourselves on that dilapidated relic of a train... ; and all of us... "homeward bound".

Code named... "Operation Olympic", the assault on the Southeast corner of Japan.., the Island of Kyushu.., was only weeks away. By early Spring.., probably late March.., the big Northern Island of Honshu.., with Japan's largest and most densely populated cities, would experience the dreaded fury of an American amphibious assault. And the citadels of Tokyo, Yokosuka, and Yokohama, would fall to that war terminating attack... , "Operation Coronet".

Designated to act as liaison, between the UDTs and General Eichelberger's Staff planning sessions at MacArthur's Manila Headquarters, Commander Draper Kauffman would later recall that, for the first time, he had become pessimistic as to whether he would come through that operation alive. Asked the planner's assessment concerning the operation, Kauffman recalled that..., "the best that we could hope for was to lose only two-thirds of our people. In other words, we had a plan... , each landing area would have ten teams... , and we'd plan on using three, and replacing them with three, and replacing them with three.......". Commenting on his own doubts that his luck was finally running out, Kauffman pondered further and repeated... , "I must say, it's the only time that I was pessimistic in the war......."

As if there were a possibility BuPers might suddenly change it's mind and, reversing our orders, issue another set... , when recalling the past 16 months and the unexpected about-face in our status... , in our lives.., Johnson and I would find ourselves speaking in a hushed manner... , even in whispers. With each "clickety clack", the train's wheels carried that crammed train further away from the Pacific coast... , and into the so called "breadbasket" of America. Passing sparsely lighted lonely farmhouses, slowing up a trace to pass through little trackside towns..., now, the fact that our thoughts and doubt concerned those who may not be returning to those remote American homes, seems only natural. Many of those "homeward bound" must have recalled the tens of thousands who wouldn't make it home, or any other place for Christmas, in 1945.

With much naive speculation as to the "atomic bomb", we knew hardly anything..! Two widely separated explosions, devastating their targets in seconds, Hiroshima and Nagasaki, had accomplished what would have taken one hell of a lot of costly missions. It worked! And thousands of American and Japanese lives had been saved. And apparently convinced the fanatical Japs not to prolong the inevitable... , to surrender! It had been readily apparent to those returning from Japan that, "Third Fleet" carrier bombers, and B-29s out of Tinian, had already persuaded those Japanese who were sane, that they were blindly pursuing a cause promulgated by medieval leadership and cultural isolation.

It is frustratingly confounding when Americans, who weren't there, not even born, or were safe in the States, criticize those who developed and authorized the bomb's use. Even FDR and Harry Truman. And find it possible to be critical of those heroic then young.... , but now aging ... , U.S. Army Airforce Fliers who, by making the actual delivery of the two bombs, saved the fathers of many of the "baby boom" generation, while risking their own. Had they attacked those Army Airforce Fliers 50+ years ago, they would have become eligible to have both legs connected separately to one of those heavy steel round weights used to solemnly confine Navy casualties to the deep! And then, after selecting a deep shark infested Pacific "gully"!

It had been repeatedly estimated by old Pacific hands, knowl-edgeable military leaders of that period, that the battle for the home islands would ultimately have caused a million casualties. History revisionists, with little or no first hand knowledge, ever anxious to sell a book or make a movie, continue to contradict those who were there with outrageous impunity. And what about the enemy.., he fought fanatically.., sometimes to the last man.., on every island that he was to defend on the U. S. route to Tokyo. The defense of the home islands was unequivocally predictable...; Japanese military and civilian losses would far exceed those of the triumphant American Landing Forces.

And those castigating the U.S. Military seem to have trouble with the estimated "million casualty" figure. With the Japanese population concentrated in the direct path of the assault forces, those coastal cities could count on being "softened up" for days in advance of the amphibious operations. That figure may well have been on the light side! Take a look at the record of pre-war.., even wartime Japan. And you see a medieval culture with an Emperor as their God. And for whom they were anxious to die.., and did! How else do you rationalize the Kamikaze phenomenon? And how many Americans lives had that medieval rationality already cost? How many additional casualties do today's "bleeding hearts" think that generation should have contributed?

It is readily acknowledged, by intelligent and educated well read students of the Pacific war, that "the bomb", as it quickly became known, in reality saved more Japanese lives than Ameri-can! Spared unprecedented Naval bombardment and carpet bomb-ing, inestimable property damage, that always preceded a full scale Pacific amphibious assault, did not take place. An operation already forming, it would have been executed within a matter of weeks.

Arriving just as the late afternoon winter darkness was de-scending over a holiday decorated Chicago, Johnson and I found that reports of a crowded station in mass confusion proved to be right on target. Faced with minutes to make the next "connec-tion", our trains being at different terminals, there was hardly time to exchange a few parting words. And we parted hurriedly. Married while on leave before "shipping out", as expected, Johnson had been distracted by the additional concerns that wartime brought to a newly married young sailor.

Speculating on his plans, he knew he had to complete his obligation to the Navy, then go back and obtain a degree at Michigan State, and finally to get on with married life. Anxious to a return to college at East Lansing, he planned to begin final work on his degree in the Fall of 1946.

Slinging my lightly packed seabag over my shoulder, like thousands of other GIs moving through the Chicago terminal two days before Christmas 1945, I took time out to confirm the "scuttlebutt" upon which we had all been depending. Checking with "Traveler's Aid", as pointed out earlier, it was confirmed that a Pittsburgh bound train could not be boarded at that terminal. Directed to the front of the building, it was understood that transportation was available from there to the "Pennsy" station.

Working my way through the "in a holiday mood" crowd, asking a civilian, he indicated my "best bet" was ...., just what I expected and obvious... , "take a cab!"

Moving too slow with the crowd, managing to get behind two fast moving Army Paratroopers, they headed for a canvass covered 2 1/2 ton truck parked near the curb loading Army personnel with their gear. Apparently organized by the Army to transport GIs between the two terminals, I made it a point not to ask whether or not the Navy was eligible. Assumptively tossing my seabag up on the truck and climbing aboard, I managed to hold on to an end seat with a view of the city through the rear flap in the canvass. Bumping across town along the cold snowy overcast Chicago streets, the city was spilling over with Christmas spirit for the first time in four years. With colorfully lighted Christmas decorations.., and sidewalks bustling with "bundled up" shoppers going in every direction... , retail business had to be booming!

Entering Penn Station on the run, and no time for a ticket counter queue, I was told that, if I moved fast, I could be on board the "Pittsburgher" when it pulled out. Less than 5 minutes to find the gate and board, it was reminiscent of the momentum Johnson and I had entering the "LA" Terminal a few days earlier. Managing to garner directions as I ran and jostled through the crowd in the direction of the gate to the Pittsburgh bound "overnighter", the train was already loaded and minutes away from departing... Passing steam hissing coaches, porters were placing the last baggage on board. And managing to slip by a conductor placing the portable step on board, climbed through the still open door of a coach near the front just as it was being secured. And followed on his heels until he finally pointed to a seat on the aisle. No time to pick up a candy bar or even a newspaper in either station, I reluctantly paid a vendor a dollar for a dry sandwich consisting of two unbuttered pieces of white bread and a slice of luncheon meat.

Barely seated before the train started to get underway, the engine began it's typical coach shuffle preparing to work it's way out of the station while the lightly clad conductors continued to slam the doors tight and shut out the cold. Within minutes, still getting settled and organizing my gear, a conductor, moving rapidly through the car, expected to pick up a ticket as he passed. And was told to collect on his next trip. And he did! Parting reluctantly with my last twenty, expecting only a few dollars change, that would take me to Pittsburgh. Muttering that this train would make a short stop in Pittsburgh, then continue on to Harrisburg, Philadelphia and finally to New York, he scowled first at the bill and then me. And grumbled something about returning with the "change". Arriving in Pittsburgh by noon the following day.. Christmas Eve.., I could expect to end up in Harrisburg late that same night. Christmas Eve could be on a crowded coach between then smokey Pittsburgh, on the West edge of the Keystone State, and the Capital in the center. Whatever sleep there was... , would be on a hard station bench. And a mid-morning Christmas Day train into Williamsport.

Even before arriving in the gray, overcast, smoke, and soot darkened downtown Pittsburgh about noon on the 24th, I had to know for certain if there were any other options. Assuring myself that there were no direct trains or buses that night, I managed to see a map of the state long enough to figure out the most direct automobile route. Mentioning that I was considering "thumbing it", I was again reminded that, with gasoline and tires in short supply, there were hardly any cars out on the highways, "you could find yourself stranded along a lonely road on Christmas Eve... , little or no traffic... , and limited chances for a "pick up." And, in 1945, there were few hotels along the over two hundred mile route through the beautiful but remote mountains.

Christmas Eve on a sooty crowded smoke filled coach, sleeping on a hard bench in a drafty cold station, and then Christmas morning on another "milk stop" local to "Billtown". "Thumbing" through the scenic snow covered mountains sounded easy.. . Not a very difficult decision!

What could have been a cold and slow "street car" ride to the end of the line, instead was a spirited half hour with Pittsburghers already warmed and charmed full with Christmas cheer. Through light traffic at the edge of the city, the almost empty trolley's last stop was a stone's throw from the Pennsylvania Turnpike entrance. At that time the only pre-war super highway in the U.S.A., the initial phase of the now completed inter-state system ended at the Carlisle, Pennsylvania interchange.... . Urged to stand just beyond his booth, with hardly any Christmas Eve traffic to stop at his toll station, the "collector" predicted a quick pick up. Even before I would stick out my thumb, he had lined up a trucker offering a ride as far as the Bedford Interchange. Following Route 220 North over winding narrow mountain stretches, and through breathtaking scenic snowy passes, the ending leg of the three thousand mile junket was in home territory. With the sky growing darker as the afternoon progressed, most travelers were already wherever they had intended to be. And settled in for the night. In a series of short hops..., the winding narrow "220" took us past familiar farms and closed country stores with old hand operated gas pumps.

In Pennsylvania, darkness arrives early on the 24th of December, one of the shortest days of the year. Especially when a winter gray sky is laden with low dark clouds and gusting swirls of blowing snow. A steady downfall piled it's feathered layers on the overhanging dark green hemlocks. Only a half century earlier, similar tall stately hemlocks made Pennsylvania number one in the world in the lumbering industry. As in a subdued black and white "Currier and Ives" Christmas card scene, sketched at every turn along the way, the thick dark green hemlock branches had begun to sag low under the weight of accumulating layers of fluffy snow. Causing them to sometimes touch the slippery roads and edges of swift icy mountain streams. For a just returning sailor, from the barren brown Southern California hills, an awakening reminder of earlier "endless mountain" winter holidays.

In the rural areas of Pennsylvania in 1945, "knocking off" early on Christmas Eve meant that folks were already settled comfortably in their homes. Or had arrived at their holiday destinations well in advance of the family's much anticipated Christmas Eve dinner hour. As years have sharpened my focus on those details, I have become increasingly aware that I cannot recall a driver that had not pulled over to offer a ride. Not wanting to interfere with any longer "hop" that may be offered, they were mostly concerned that they were only going a short distance.., a mile or so.... Almost never declining, I elected to pass up a ride only when it appeared the driver's destination was just too close..., or an old truck too slow.

Having thumbed from Coronado to "LA" along the Pacific Coast only days earlier, the contrast of the folks in the hills of Penn's Woods, as opposed to those along the ocean road of Southern California, was never more evident than on that Christmas Eve. A short noisy ride was offered by a farmer, driving his little 1936 black Ford truck with a wire screened "bed", delivering last minute "live" Christmas turkeys to rural customers. Several miles before arriving in Altoona, I half listened and partially dozed through a warm comfortable half hour with a concerned and dedicated Minister. As the hour grew near for the traditional Christmas Eve candlelight service, the pastor hurried to make certain that his country church's coal fired furnace was not "banked", and his sanctuary cold.

Fresh revelations, of recently released American POWs, prompted me to ask his reaction, as a minister, to those stories.

Particularly of the accounts of brutal treatment and starvation..,
the atrocities. The POW's emaciated condition when found in
camps on Honshu, Formosa and China. And those uncovered a
few months earlier by U.S. Occupation Forces in POW camps... ,
at Zentsuji, Kawasaki, Hakodate, Osaka, Kobe, Hieji, Fuuoka
etc., etc.. . As a minister, how did he react to those stories?

Beginning with the early reports filtering back from Bataan,
Corregidor, Wake, Guam, Singapore, Hong Kong, the first forward bases to surrender, from December 7th on, Americans
agonized over the treatment of their POWs by the Japanese. More
recently, an account of a Naval Commander's POW experience, as
related to his son who lived in Japan for a number of years
beginning in 1956, had been deliberately withheld at the State
Department's request during his son's tour in that country as a
Naval Attache.

Before the son embarked to take up his post in Japan, recalling
his POW experiences, his elderly father's counsel had been to...,
"not be taken in".

Returning briefly again to Japan a number of years later, the
POW's son was curious to see if there had been any change in
Japanese sentiment. Again he did not divulge his father's wartime POW status to his Japanese acquaintances. Finally mentioning his private apprehension to a long time American resident
of Tokyo, her reply summed up the cultural animosity toward the
West and particularly the U.S.;

"It would have made little difference. They would have replied
either that my Father's experience was the fault of the Japanese
Army, or that those were events of which they had no cognizance."
Further, the friend described the Japanese as, "trying to rewrite
history. Instead of teaching young people about the events of the
Second World War in the Pacific, they were trying to avoid the
issue or to recast it completely." The author had noted poignantly
.........., "there are many living with the scars that refute those
altered history books. But when they die, who will refute the
books then?"

Piously assuming the usual admonishment to be "forgiving"
etc., the minister was obviously more distracted with his problem
of the moment... , that of the church's sexton who may be
celebrating early. And anxious to make certain that his
congregation's Christmas Eve service would be warm and comfortable. To see that it went off without a hitch.

Incensed....., before allowing the subject to switch, waiting to
get my point across, my annoyed observation was, "the Japs were
lucky that they picked Christian U.S.A. to attack."

Finally in very familiar territory, a recognizable landmark at
every turn, it was all "down hill". A most relaxing stint on that

final leg came with a discharged Navy man, also just having arrived home on "terminal leave", happily on his way to meet his girl friend. Cautioning concern... , paying attention to the sparse traffic... , the ex-sailor drove several miles out of his way... , miles beyond his destination... , in order to drop me in an area where he was certain I would have a better shot at passing traffic.

The hour was late, and having switched directions again, the cutting wind blew gusts of thick falling snow against the wind-shield. Making visibility more difficult, the clogged wipers needed to be cleaned of accumulating ice and snow periodically.

Returning from a last minute Christmas Eve delivery to a customer located West of Lock Haven, at Dunnstown a furniture store driver pulled over and opened the door of his dray. With almost no traffic on the last few miles, we passed close to the familiar tobacco sheds and old barns, with freshly painted "Redman" tobacco signs, that bordered the roads of the rural Clinton County countryside... . Passing quickly through "buttoned up" Avis, down the Allegheny Street hill in Jersey Shore and finally through much decorated Newberry, we passed Bowman Field into Williamsport before encountering an automobile along Fourth Street just before Maynard.

Dropped off at the South curb of Fourth Street and Trinity Place... , under the street light on that familiar corner in front of 835 W. Fourth... , it took only a quick minute to face Trinity with it's familiar high steeple, big clock, and usual Christmas decorations. Most likely one of my favorite ministers of all time, the Reverend J. Moulton Thomas, would be presiding at the Christmas Eve Communion Service. And Choir Master Gordon Breary's Boys Choir may even be singing the carols that Christmas Eve... .. Wearing a white surplice over a black cassock, a high starched stiff collar over a flowing silk tie, only a few years earlier I had earned a few bucks as a Trinity Choir boy. And remembered Gordon Breary as a perfectionist taskmaster.. , someone that subjected us to an early and positive influence with his relentless discipline. With all of the choir practices and demands on a very young boy's time, there had to have been something more interesting than a few occasional coins to keep them coming back. Along with the iron mandates of mothers, who saw it as a very noble youthful pursuit for their sons, there was the additional incentive provided by Trinity's second story gymnasium, and the opportunity to play a lot of basketball even in the coldest or wettest weather.

Having last called "4423" from a busy phone booth in Kansas City, the folks at home had been expecting me to arrive at any time. But when the hour had turned late and the weather more uncertain, they would become less expectant. And with the radio regularly relating stories of overtaxed railroad traffic, and jammed terminals all across the country, they had become convinced it would be sometime on the 25th... , perhaps an early train out of Harrisburg.

Having made up my mind, someplace between San Diego and Chicago, I had already resolved that the first stop would be with the pretty "Mountain Beach" lifeguard whose "scented" blue envelopes had overflowed "mail calls" for many months. And, to attend the Midshipman School commissioning exercises in the drill hall at Notre Dame, switching trains many times enroute, had endured several days on dirty coaches when traveling out to Indiana. Wherever the ship dropped the "hook", long enough for the Fleet Post Office to find us, a batch of those light thin special overseas envelopes were carried on board in big canvass bags. Apparently having somewhere been dunked and salvaged from the "drink", a few were even a little soggy when they arrived. And having also called "4452", from that same busy railroad station phone booth, the clearing weather in Kansas City provided a little momentary optimism.

And in response to "when??", guessed ... , "Christmas Eve for sure!"

Almost 2200 now, the temperature had dropped considerably. Chilled, wearing the same thin worn khakis and Brax's "foul weather" jacket, I slogged through the snow up the walk to the big stone house that had overlooked Trinity, Way's Garden and the Park Hotel for as long as anyone could remember. Flurries of blowing snow and piercing wind, gusting across the Ways Garden corner, momentarily caught my seabag... . Bone tired, I barely dodged a fleeting flirtation with an untimely coup de grace by dropping it, just as I cleared the top of the stone steps.

Crossing the wide familiar stone porch, and twisting the entrance "knocker", after a tense and unreasonable long wait, a sailor's most ardent expectation, prettily dressed in black, pulled aside the filmy curtain of the adjacent bay window. And the icy glass pane lit up with the same slow gentle smile, of the pretty "life guard", that had completely destroyed my "freestyle" a couple of Summers earlier.

Both her mother and dad were there... , and all three came to open the door. Instantly cozy warm, once inside, I dropped the traveled and soiled white seabag in the corner on the foyer floor. The warmth... , so penetrating ... , disarmingly so.. , and relaxing.. . So relaxing.. , the type that can, fleetingly deprive you of your strength, make you feel weak. The quiet softness.. , enveloping warmth.. , of a peaceful world.

Passing up a roaring fire in the parlor hearth, going directly from the front to the back of the house, and the enormous kitchen, while her seemingly always busy and thoughtful mother made a pot of hot chocolate, we sat around the table catching up on the past week. With enormous pots, pans, and utensils hanging over the big work table, still the relatively huge restaurant size kitchen always seemed to invitingly comfortable. After a week of, getting on and off of drafty, barely heated passenger coaches, the direct warmth, coming from the glow of the big old fashioned iron kitchen range, was just the ticket to finally roust out the cold that thought it found a permanent home in my fatigued bones.

Returning with cups of cocoa to the intimateness of the Christmas tree and hearth lighted parlor, the four of us settled into the two worn "overstuffed" sofas in front of a fire of damp hissing logs and leaping flames licking up into the chimney of the immense stone hearth. Stacked next it, enough logs to last well into the next year... , 1946. Hit by an almost immediate onset of a kind of relaxed drowsiness, the siren song of closed eyes and sleep was quickly rejected by the lighthearted nervous "chit chat' that only a long separation will educe. Stretching out deep into the sofa to reach the ottoman, the blazing flames were cut off by a tired pair of salt water stained "sand shoes". Having been soaked repeatedly, they looked, as they felt, to be molded to my feet. A passing urge to kick 'em off was quickly forgotten when I remembered they hadn't been removed for a week. Thinking better of it... , I relaxed a little deeper into that old sofa.

Later.. , as the hands of the clock edged around and approached twelve.. , and then passed into Christmas Day.. , outside.. , the rapidly dropping temperature painted frosty windows with lighted wintry scenes. Seasonally lighted "Billtown" homes stood in awesome contrast to the bombed and burned out buildings... , and miles of devastation... , witnessed only a few weeks earlier.

Though the hands of the parlor's "tall clock" had continued their inexorable chase... , time did stand still. But, only for a measureless seeming minuscule of time.

And it was early Christmas morning, and a "silent night" of clearing skies had settled over "Billtown". Trudging that final mile past familiar landmarks and houses, the snow, blowing from sagging tree branches, filtered down through the crystal cold air. As they had been for years, dimly lit and occasionally broken sidewalks had been pushed up a little further as the emerging roots of the huge old shade trees grew bigger and older. Undoubtedly a little more uneven than when following that same route on the way home, from school or practices, on countless occasions in similar weather.

Catching a first glimpse of my parent's brightly lit and warmly decorated home from the entrance steps, the Christmas tree, being in it's usual corner, everything appeared to be in order. It could have been ten years earlier.

Pushing open the unlocked door, in making my well past midnight entrance, literally stumbled over the seabag. With a new set of just acquired chills and shivers, compliments of a biting wind that followed the last few blocks, the past week took it's one last parting shot.

With the abating excitement of pent up anticipation, and bottomless fatigue, brought about by a week of steady travel aboard scarcely heated trains, apparently the combination had taken that moment for the physical culmination of that non-stop trek. As could be counted on, it promptly elicited a concerned parent's suggestion that, "a good night's sleep might be a good idea."

"Hey! By gosh by golly…., it was time for mistletoe and holly…!

It was Christmas Day…….., 1945.

CHAPTER XI.

"OPERATION REMEMBER"

In 1802 the United States's growing maritime importance was noted by an observer in French New Orleans: "In front of the city and along the quays there are at this moment fifty five American ships to ten French...." After James Monroe signed the treaty concluding the "Louisiana Purchase", Napoleon Bonaparte, grasping the great significance of the purchase, said: "This accession of territory confirms forever the power of the United States, and I have just given England a maritime rival that sooner or later will lay low her pride."

In May 1957, the Navy League of New York City, joined by the City's Mayor, concluded that there was still time to honor a number.. 50 in all.. of the Naval leaders "that made the difference" in World War II. Designated "Operation Remember", it would be a last reunion for many of WWII's greatest heroes.

The person most responsible, the person whose original idea brought about the memorable event, was a Reserve Rear Admiral by the name of Jack Berger. As the owner of Madison Square Garden and The Plaza Hotel, Berger carried a lot of weight in New York City. Along with several others with three and four star rank, to pick those to be honored that night, he sought the advice of Admirals Arleigh A. "30 Knot" Burke and Robert B. "Mick" Carney. The Mayor of the city, acknowledging his pleasure, handed out a record number of "keys to the city" on that morning preceding the evening dinner at the Waldorf.

Those early post WWII years would occasion an opportunity to be in touch with Captain Draper Kauffman, a "UDT" officer, with whom I had become associated during the war. After being ordered to inactive duty by the Navy in 1946, and having acquired a degree at the Wharton School of The University of Pennsylvania in February 1948, most of my employment time after the war had been spent with Philadelphia headquartered, The Atlantic Refining Company. Having retained a Reserve Commission, only weeks before Kauffman had phoned concerning an unclassified assignment that he felt would be enhanced by someone with a UDT background and an oil company affiliation.

Kauffman, then a Captain, assigned as an attache to the Secretary of the Navy, Thomas S. Gates Jr., expressed the Navy's apparent concern with the rapid loss of U.S. Merchant Marine ships flying the "stars and stripes". And, particularly the loss of tankers! Many former American flag tankers were showing up on the "high seas" flying the Greece flag and concentrated in the ownership of a Greek shipping tycoon by the name of Aristotle Onassis. Adopted for use by Americans as well, in order to compete in world trade, these were "flags of convenience". For the use of U.S. shippers precluded from competing due to high operating costs.

And it was becoming increasingly evident that American ship building contracts were also moving overseas for the same cost saving reasons. The United States Navy was becoming concerned that American shipping would not be available to it in the event of another crisis comparable to that of WWII. And building a Maritime tanker force to support war time requirements was an objective that particularly implicated the Navy.

This led to speculation that these "flag of convenience" ships could be commandeered in an emergency... , in U.S. ports, on the "high seas", and in foreign... , even enemy ports.

With those objectives, it would require that the Navy be prepared to have trained personnel available to (1.) seize the ships and dispose of their crews and (2.) have trained boarding crews available to man the ships, get them underway, and back into U.S. hands. And, apparently the area, which the Secretary and Kauffman were exploring, involved the clandestine use of the UDTs.

Another consideration, the establishment of access to facilities permitting fast direct replenishment of "Bunker C" and other fuels to Navy ships directly from coastal refineries.

In a discourse concerning WWII several years earlier, one of the subjects being UDT operations, Colonel Dwight Colley had been made aware of the legendary Draper Kauffman. Eager to assist in such matters, Colley, an Atlantic V.P., immediately referred me to Harry G. Schad, Atlantic's Vice President of Transportation.

Stiffly erect, with his closely clipped haircut and military bearing, Colonel Dwight T. Colley, Atlantic's tenacious Marketing Vice President was not held in great esteem by those who had grown "lackadaisical" as a result off their wartime sired lethargy. Serving as the very enthusing head of an aggressive Atlantic Marketing Division.. , then recognized as one of the industry's finest, he was most highly regarded by many returning Atlantic WWII veterans. And as a recognized Oil Industry leader, Colley was a personal inspiration to many.

A modest and private person, as is often the case, those particulars of his wartime military achievements were often referred to, sometimes rather inaccurately, even by those involved in World War II history.

An indication of those WWII encounters was well documented

in the biography of George S. Patton, Jr. In a Third Army operation which would eventuate in the capture of Metz, and release of two armored divisions, the Fourth and the Sixth, the mission was to blast away to cause the rupture of the Siegfried Line leading to the subsequent assault on the Rhine River. The supply situation.. , rations, gasoline and ammunition... , was exceptionally bad and the general staff was contemplating every effort to ameliorate the consequence. As reported in Patton's Diary, the record of Colonel Colley is embodied in his Distinguished Service Cross citation which reads as follows:

"On the 25th of October 1944, Colonel D. T. Colley's 104th Infantry Regiment of the 26th Division made an attack. They were about 3/4 successful as a portion of the hill remained still in enemy possession. However, the Commanding General (Paul) thought that they had been allowed sufficient opportunity and directed other Regiments to take over the assault as of 1800. Colley got wind of this at about 1300, went up to his leading Battalion Officers and told them that the honor of their Regiment did not permit them to turn over an incomplete job. He stated that he would lead the assault himself which he did with great gallantry. The position was taken, but Colley was shot in the right shoulder, with the bullet progressing through both lungs and emerging from the lower part of the left lung, miraculously missing the heart and blood vessels on their way."

Awarded his second Distinguished Service Cross by General Patton, Dwight T. Colley was presented with an Oak Leaf Cluster to add to that which he had won in World War I. After a period of hospitalization and a complete recovery, D.T. Colley, returned at his own request to command a Regiment. Quite an unusual and unique honor, the Colonel had won both the Distinguished Service Cross and the Purple Heart in both World Wars. A staunch testimony to the strength and fortitude of the character of the individual who headed up Atlantic's Marketing Department.

Schad took the time to provide a good briefing on the dilemma facing his tanker business. Obviously the dollars mentioned were those of the period.. , quite a difference as compared with those of today. Schad's 1957 assessment was:

"The cost of building ships in foreign countries is much lower than in the United States, and the costs of operating ships under foreign flags are considerably lower than under our own flag. As to building costs, for example, the larger ships cost us almost $ 9 3/4 million in the United States. A comparable ship constructed overseas would cost considerably less, but still about $ 7 million. Unless this course is followed, we could not be competitive in the utilization of foreign crude oils and product movement outside the

United States. Under the law, only an American flag vessel can operate between ports in the United States."

It was during World War II that Kauffman, along with Commander Jack Koehler, a few short years later an Assistant Secretary of the Navy in the Eisenhower Administration, who would crucially drive my Navy career. In the course of our phone conversation, Kauffman, then stationed in Washington, touched on the upcoming event. Sensing my admiration for those being honored, he undertook to set aside one of the much sought after tickets.

My early initial impression had been that it was to be a UDT event. Explained in more detail, it was plainly not just a run-of-the-mill "get together" reunion... Many of the special now elderly officers to be honored that night may never see each other again. With a typical of the times inflexible employer, a wife and two small children, although privately uncertain, I tentatively accepted anyway. As the date grew closer, when Kauffman sent over a copy of the program, it became clear that it would be a noteworthy event not to be missed. Tickled to have an invitation, I had to find a way to get over to New York City on that night.

Though, as a UDT, made aware of the many stories surrounding the legendary Kauffman as early as 1944, we first became personally acquainted on Maui early in 1945. And continued to cross paths. While I pursued a course of employment with Atlantic Refining, he had finally been cleared to carry on with his long endeavor, beginning with graduation from The Naval Academy in 1933, to carve out a "regular Navy" career. At the commencement of the Korean crisis, along with numerous others, the Navy ordered Reserves to "update" their medical history and "qualification jacket", "up date" their "shots", and to interview concerning orders to "active duty". As another "hitch" seemed to be inevitable, thoughts of returning to the UDTs obliged me to talk to Kauffman and consider becoming a career sailor.

At our initial 1945 encounter, having just flown over to Maui from Pearl, Kauffman walked into Koehler's tent just in time to overhear my restive inquiry into a prompt transfer of duty to the fleet. And had overheard my explanation to Koehler that, "as far as I can tell, I'm as good a swimmer as there is in the UDTs." And he was surprised to hear my response to Koehler's question on demolition expertise, when I countered with, "I make up all of the `firing assemblies'.. .., most of the others don't know how!" And that's what really concerned Kauffman.

With the stirring dispatches of the "skirmishes" of the Third and Fifth Fleets in the Western Pacific, it was my concern that the best action of the Pacific war was being missed. It was just a coincidence that Commander Koehler brought Kauffman into our discussion. Having just been given the additional assignment of heading up Admiral Kelly Turner's "Planning Staff" for UDT Operations, Kauffman joined Koehler in blending enthusiasm with persuasion to sparingly divulge future UDT operations. Both were in accord in suggesting, "the Navy would need all of the trained UDT'S available." In addition to Formosa, China, Iwo and Okinawa, I would learn many years later that they had been in the midst of discussing personnel logistics surrounding Turner's plan for the long awaited amphibious operations against the "homeland"... , Japan itself. Obviously they had "Operation Olympic" and "Operation Coronet" in mind... , the invasion of Kyushu in October-November 1945.. , and in March 1946, Honshu... . When it also became recognized that the Navy estimated UDT casualties for those operations to be in the neighborhood of 60% to 70%, the reason for their concern likewise became clear. Again... , years later... , we had occasion to remind each other of those earlier discussions.

In November and December 1945, after all UDTs had returned to their new base on Coronado Island, Kauffman would do his utmost to recruit officers to remain in the regular Navy and the UDTS. Alone, he would wryly remind me of our earlier encounter and request for duty with the Fleet.

But "Operation Remember" was for a very special reunion of a special group... , the highest ranking World War II Navy and Marine Corps Officers. Kauffman graciously gave the impression that, as a Flag Officer Aide to the Secretary of the Navy, he had been pleased to be able to say to the Secretary that one of the WWII UDTs was in attendance that night.

The fifty World War II four and three star Navy Admirals and Marine Corps Generals had been chosen for being... , "the officers it was felt had been largely responsible for the leadership in the magnificent successes of the Navy and the Marine Corp in the recent conflict....". The Navy League had relied on the advice and counsel of the then active duty Admirals... Arleigh "30 knot" Burke and Robert B. "Mick" Carney... Both men had also attained their "star" rank during World War II.

Having succeeded Secretary Charles S. Thomas, who had served as Secretary of the Navy from May 3, 1954 to April 1, 1957, Gates held that cabinet post, under President Dwight D. Eisenhower, from April 1, 1957 through June 8, 1959. And then succeeded Deputy Secretary of Defense Donald A. Quarles, who had also served under Eisenhower from May 1957 through April 30, 1959. Deputy Secretary of Defense Tom Gates held that job through December 1, 1959. And on December 2, 1959, he succeeded Niel H. McElroy as Eisenhower's third Secretary of Defense. The other being Charles E. Wilson. Wilson, former Presi-

dent of General Motors Corporation, to differentiate him from
"Electric Charlie", President of the General Electric Company,
was popularly known as "Engine Charlie".

Although Secretary of the Navy for just one month, Thomas
Gates, Jr. was appropriately asked by the New York City Council
of the Navy League to address those in attendance that night at
the Waldorf. And, according to witnesses, he completed five
different drafts of his speech before, still not being satisfied, tore
up a fifth draft copy on the plane to New York City. And in that
last hour of his flight, ended up jotting down his most personal
thoughts on a yellow pad.

Many of those that the committee had selected had become
household "names' in the early `40s. On the Navy side this
included such officers as Admirals Chester W. Nimitz, William F.
"Bull" Halsey, Jr., Raymond A. Spruance, Thomas C. Hart, Alan
G. Kirk, and from the Marine Corps, Generals Holland M. Smith,
Harry Schmidt, Roy S. Geiger, Graves, and Erskine. Along with
the fifty now elderly distinguished officers, as the principal
speaker, Gates was seated near the center of the long dais along
the west wall of the Waldorf's mammoth ballroom. Holding one of
New York's famous "ticker tape" parades up Broadway, earlier in
the day the Mayor of the city had presented each of the fifty
"guests of honor" with a key to the "Big Apple".

In most large banquet rooms, a dais with sixty people sounds
incredible. But it didn't appear to be a problem that night at the
"Waldorf" where the waiters moved as fast as they talked and
often seemed to get lost. Along with others that evening, I
discovered a reason for not ordering a drink from a Waldorf
banquet room table. Apparently it was not expected that the
waiters should account for the "change".

Earlier in the day, before the formalities of the evening had
begun, the reunion committee had provided a reception permitting the honorees private time to spend together and to renew old
friendships. Reminiscing in a language they had created out of
the fraternity of their war experiences... , they had the time of
their lives. A language hardly understood outside the Naval
Fraternity... , so much could be left unsaid. And yet, as they
engaged each other in their personal recollections of those history
making times, these officers easily understood.

Deeply appreciative of the Navy League's testimonial and the
consideration tendered them in planning this event, according to
observers, there were deep emotional reactions on the part of
these men who thought that they had been forgotten.

Forgotten.... ! Not this time.... !

Not as portrayed by that noted British author and writer,
Rudyard Kipling. Recognized for having so often romanticized

the life of the British Soldier, Kipling, who died in 1836, had legendized the plight of the forgotten warrior.. , and as he particularly spelled it out in the last verse of his poem "Tommy"...;

For it's Tommy this, an Tommy that, an'
"Chuck him out the brute!"

But it's "Savior of 'is country," when the
guns begin to shoot;

Yes it's Tommy this, an Tommy that, an'
anything you please;

But Tommy ain't a bloomin fool— you bet
that Tommy sees!

Only a few years earlier, after an extraordinary lifetime of service to their country, they had been ordered to inactive duty. And, in the turmoil of the post war demilitarization with millions returning to civilian life, into the "black hole" of fading memories, with little recognition, they had simply slipped away from the public view. As it turned out... , the Navy League testimonial was most meaningful and important to these genuine American heroes. And it was appropriate that they should finally be honored.

And there were times, during Gates' speech, when their deep seeded feelings could no longer be withheld. Or go undetected during the reunion of these supposedly "calloused" veterans of the Pacific battles.. . And then their eyes, of these old comrades-in-arms, would glisten with moisture. As the Secretary's "looking back" address roused strong emotions, handkerchiefs "popped" like signal flags from the Missouri's "flag bag". A University of Pennsylvania graduate, a World War II Navy Veteran himself, young Tom Gates had served as a Lieutenant, in Naval Aviation Intelligence and as an Admiral's Aide, aboard a Carrier. As was certainly the case of other World War II Navy men in the room that night, these Senior Officers were Gate's heroes. And like so many that filled the Waldorf's Ballroom, he also had a bad case of nostalgia for these individuals and those dark times of faded khakis and sea soaked "sand shoes" under an unrelenting hot Pacific sun.

Gates made an all out effort to make it an unforgettable tribute to the honorees. Never fully satisfied with the speech that finally evolved on the plane between Washington and New York, still and all, it was the result of the diligent personal effort of the Secretary himself... , his own private thoughts and words. And from his inner most depths he poured out his heart. A chronology of Naval WWII highlights, never really written as a speech, merely his reference notes, as written and presented by Tom Gates on that night in the Waldorf Astoria Ballroom at "Operation Remember", reads as follows:

"THIS IS 'OPERATION REMEMBER'. TODAY THE JUNGLE GROWS HIGH OVER GUADALCANAL. A LONE FISHERMAN WALKS OMAHA BEACH. ANZIO IS REBUILT. ESPIRITU SANTO MEANS ONLY IT'S ENGLISH TRANSLATION, AND TRUK IS AGAIN A LONELY ATOLL. THE WORLD FORGETS QUICKLY. MEN WHO WERE THERE REMEMBER, AND THERE WERE MILLIONS OF THEM. THOSE WHO WERE THERE WILL NEVER FORGET THE FLARES OF THE EARLY TORPEDO ATTACKS, THE HASTILY BUILT BEER PLACES THAT CAME LATER, THE SMELL OF THE DEAD, THE JUNGLE ROT OF THE SOLOMONS, THE PERFECTION OF THE GERMAN ....AND THE KAMIKAZE, THE STORIES THAT GROW BETTER WITH THE YEARS, THE FRIENDSHIPS DEEPER THAN ANY, THE BRIDGE GAMES THAT CHANGED AS THE REGULAR MEMBERS DID NOT RETURN, THE BLOODY BEACHES OF TARAWA, THE THRILL OF THE HALSEY "GET MOVING TONIGHT" DISPATCHES, THE CAREFUL PLANNING OF SPRUANCE.

THE CONFIDENCE INSTILLED BY THE BRILLIANCE AND CALM OF NIMITZ, THE FLEET "LIT UP" BY MITSCHER WHOM THE PILOTS LOVED, THE DREAM OF A LIFETIME WHEN OLENDORF CROSSED THE "T" AT SURIGAO, THE FLAG AT IWO, THE BOYS IN THE WATER, THE NAMES "ENTERPRISE", "LEX"", "YORKTOWN", "SOUTH DAKOTA", "SALT LAKE CITY", "BOISE", "O'BANNION"; THOSE OF BOB VANDERGRIFT, "HOWLIN' MAD" SMITH, McCAIN, "BUTCH" O'HARE, "KILLER" KANE, ERSKINE AND CATES, THOSE OF CORAL SEA AND MIDWAY, THE SIX MARINE DIVISIONS, "SCRATCH ONE FLAT TOP", "SLOT", "SEND US MORE JAPS". THE "TURKEY SHOOT", THE "CAN- DO, WILL, OR DO" SEABEES, THE NAZIS, THE NIPS, GREATER EAST ASIA CO- PROSPERITY SPHERE, THE RISING SUN, THE SWASTIKA. THOSE WHO WERE THERE SAY, "THESE THINGS I LIVED, THESE DAYS TAUGHT ME THE LOVE OF GOD". THESE DAYS BROUGHT OUT OF THE SMOKE AND DEATH OF PEARL HARBOR THE GREATEST FORCE ON EARTH, THE INGENUITY AND THE RESOURCES OF AMERICA TO PRODUCE THE GREATEST POWER EVER DEVISED, AND THE UNITED STATES OF AMERICA RODE THE AIRWAYS AND THE SEAWAYS OF THE EARTH.

THESE FORCES WERE LED BY MEN, MEN TRAINED FOR

*YEARS, MEN WHO EXISTED FOR JUST SUCH AN EMER-
GENCY. IT WAS THEIR REASON FOR BEING, THE REASON
FOR THEIR SERVICES TO EXIST. LET US NEVER FORGET
THE PURPOSE OF THE MILITARY IS TO FIGHT TO WIN
WARS. MANY OF THOSE MEN ARE HERE. COMBAT AND
THE STRAIN OF WAR TOOK MANY OF THEIR CONTEMPO-
RARIES. THEY ARE THE EPITOME OF THE MOST PRICE-
LESS COMMODITY OF FREEDOM...., LEADERSHIP. WE
ARE INCLINED THESE DAYS, AS A RESULT OF SOME OF
OUR EXPERIENCES IN WAR, TO THINK PRIMARILY OF
VICTORY IN TERMS OF QUANTITATIVE SUPERIORITY IN
TERMS OF MEN, SHIPS, AND PLANES, IN RESOURCES,
MONEY, AND MUNITIONS.*

*REMEMBER THE "TROJAN" RESPONSE FROM MINE,
FACTORY, AND FARM...., A CARDINAL FACTOR IN NAVAL
SUCCESS, THE AMAZING WARTIME PRODUCTION IN
SHIPS, PLANES, AND GUNS, THE GENIUS OF OUR ENGI-
NEERS, SCIENTISTS, MECHANICS, AND LABORERS. MILI-
TARY SUCCESS IS LIKEWISE DEPENDENT MORE AND
MORE ON NEW DEVELOPMENTS AND NEW TECHNIQUES,
OR, ESPECIALLY NOW DAYS, ON ACHIEVEMENTS IN SCI-
ENCE AND ENGINEERING.*

*REMEMBER THE SUPERIORITY OF CARRIER WARFARE,
WHICH SPEARHEADED THE WAR IN THE PACIFIC, ONE OF
THE GREAT ACHIEVEMENTS IN THE HISTORY OF MOD-
ERN WARFARE, AMPHIBIOUS FORCES PERFECTED TO A
DEGREE HITHERTO TO UNIMAGINABLE, INCOMPARABLE
SUBMARINE FORCES, WHICH ALMOST SINGLE HANDED
"STRANGLED" THE JAPANESE, FANTASTICALLY FLEX-
IBLE AND RESPONSIVE LOGISTIC FORCES, UNDERWAY
REPLENISHMENT, THE BIRTH OF THE "HUNTER KILLER"
TEAMS.. ."SIGHTED SUB.. SANK SAME", THE BIRTH OF
THE "UNDERWATER DEMOLITION TEAMS"— THE "UDTs",
FANTASTICALLY INGENIOUS, INDEED, ARE THESE TECH-
NIQUES AND DEVELOPMENTS, JUST AS ARE THOSE OF
THE ATOM, THE MISSILE AND THE JET.*

*THE UNITED STATES AND THE FREE WORLD LIKEWISE
IS RICHLY ENDOWED BY NATURAL RESOURCES. THE
WORLD HAS NEVER SEEN THE LIKES OF OUR WEALTH
AND PRODUCTIVITY, YET THESE MATERIAL THINGS PALE
TO RELATIVE UNIMPORTANT WITHOUT LEADERSHIP.
THE INSPIRATIONAL LEADERSHIP OF A SERGEANT DI-
RECTING A SQUAD OF MARINES OR THE BRILLIANT LEAD-
ERSHIP OF AN ADMIRAL DIRECTING A TASK FORCE. THIS
IS THE ESSENTIAL INGREDIENT ABOVE ALL ELSE IN
VICTORY. THOSE HERE TONIGHT ARE REPRESENTATIVE*

OF THE LEADERSHIP WHICH LED OUR COUNTRY IN IT'S EXPLOITATION OF GLOBAL SEAPOWER TO A DEGREE UNMATCHED AT ANY OTHER TIME IN OUR HISTORY. THEY ARE REPRESENTATIVE OF THE MEN WHO FILLED THE RANKS AND MANNED THE SHIPS IN THE MAGNIFICENT MANNER REQUIRED, WHICH CHARACTERIZED OUR WORLD WAR II NAVY. THROUGHOUT THE WAR, THEIR LEADERSHIP EMPLOYED OUR BALANCED FLEETS IN SUCH A MANNER AS TO EXPLOIT FULLY THE ABILITY OF THE NAVY TO CONCENTRATE NAVAL POWER AT ANY DESIRED POINT IN SUCH A MANNER AS TO OVERWHELM THE DEFENSE AT THE POINT OF CONTACT. THIS LEADERSHIP DEMONSTRATED THE CAPABILITY OF SEAPOWER TO MAKE USE OF THE PRINCIPALS OF MOBILITY, CONCENTRATION, AND ECONOMY OF FORCE TO A DEGREE APPROACHING THE ULTIMATE.

MODERN WEAPONS ARE CHANGING IN APPEARANCE AND THE MEANS OF APPLICATION, BUT THE PRINCIPALS OF APPLICATION ARE UNCHANGED. THESE PRINCIPALS GUIDE OUR LEADERS TODAY, RADFORD, "30 KNOTT" BURKE', PATE.

THEY WILL GUIDE OUR LEADERS OF TOMORROW. THUS THEY HAVE PLAYED A VITAL PART, NOT ONLY IN HISTORY BUT IN THE FUTURE, WHICH IS FULL OF PROMISE BECAUSE OF THE STRENGTH AND THE WILL OF ALL THE FREE PEOPLE OF THE WESTERN WORLD, AN OCEANIC CONFEDERACY CEMENTED TOGETHER BY SEAPOWER.

FOR YOUR CONTRIBUTION TO THE GLORIOUS PAST AND THE GREAT FUTURE, WE THANK YOU AND SALUTE YOU."

The standing applause was as good as it gets!!

It would not have been a surprise if the entire room, having risen to their feet... , would let loose with three tumultuous... "Hip! Hip! Hoorays!....", and thrown the Waldorf's chairs high into the air.

Neither Gates, nor anyone else, could make a contemporary audience comprehend that speech today. Even the most patient would barely comprehend it's meaning... , it's significance.

It might be compared to that 1930's-40's college burlesque that majored in the then current popular expression, and went something like this:

> "She's got `pink tooth brush',
> She's got the 'hush hush'
> Her 'B O' keeps her friends away
>
> She's in no 'date book',
> She's got that 'painted look'
> etc. ...."

She's just an old hag,
With a mid-section sag,
She's just a... Yale.. Bulldog bag!'"

With all those old "bromides", no longer in use after so many years. , not contemporary slang... , that ancient 1930's ditty looses most of it's humor. Not even understandable...., pure "Greek" to a contemporary audience!

Whether or not you thought that was an earthquake of a speech that evening at the Waldorf, an 8.5 on the "Richter Scale", was the wholly subjective viewpoint of each individual in attendance. Like the private conversations of those before and during dinner, there was so much unstated. And a single word, a place, an "operation", the name of a ship or division, a quotation, a person's name... , was a code that, because of the special personal perspective of most in attendance that night in 1957, triggered their own private explication. Ever and again, just a couple of those words, written and softly spoken... , almost reverently... , by Gates that night, would trigger volumes of subjective history.

On it's surface, much of the speech appears to be nothing more than a disconnected word or an abbreviated sentence; but delivered with a pause, allowing the listener to reflect on his own private perceptions, would evoke a vignette of proportions conceived privately by each individual. With the predominantly Navy audience, it packed a "hell of a wallop". They loved it.

As President of the University of Pennsylvania, Thomas S. Gates' father presided over the 1740 institution ... , the nation's first University... , when the first V-12s entered Penn. And when many of those same men returned to Philadelphia in the Fall of 1946, the senior Gates had already retired to assume the newly created post of Chairman of The University. And continued to serve in that capacity until he suddenly passed away on April 8, 1948. In an after dinner conversation with Tom Jr., it was not difficult for him to relate his father's interest in the Naval V-12 unit. And he had been made particularly aware of those times when his father stood along the side of Captain Stevens on the cool green grass within the high stands and brick walls of venerated Franklin Field. Of the occasions when he reviewed the Battalion on parade under a bright Summer sun or on a brisk Autumn morning.

Wearing his familiar light cord suit, and protected from the sun's rays by only his 1930's style broad brimmed Panama hat, like the Naval Officers at his side, he stood erect in the center of the breezeless two tiered brick stadium to review Penn's sailors on a Saturday at high noon. In "undress whites", scrubbed canvass "leggin's", squared white hats and "two blocked" black scarfs, the "Quaker" sailors marched to Navy and Penn music played by their own Navy band. Coming out to West Philadelphia to review the Battalion from the South Broad Street Navy Yard , Rear Admiral Milo F. Draemel, U.S.N., Commandant 4th Naval District, also took his place along the side of the University's President and the Commanding Officer of the unit ... .

As a matter of interest, Rear Admiral Milo F. Draemel, USNA '06, was a classmate and close friend of the cantankerous Admiral John H. Towers, the Navy's number one pilot. And at that particular time, as Deputy CINCPAC to Admiral Chester W. Nimitz, Towers held one of the highest posts in the wartime Navy. Later, he would replace Nimitz as the Commander in Chief Pacific Fleet.

At the time of the graduation of that uncharacteristic "veteran" "Class of `48", George McClelland, who as Provost, had first welcomed the V-12s to Penn, and by then elevated to the post of President of the University, was fittingly the signatory to their diplomas.

CHAPTER XII.

NAVY DAY 1945

"Navies do not dispense with fortifications nor with armies, but when wisely handled they may save the country the strain which comes when these have to be called into play."
Alfred Thayer Mahan; The Influence of Seapower
Upon the French Revolution
and Empire, 1892.

Over on Maui, the few remaining UDTs were busy tearing down the tents that had comprised their secret base on the side of Mount Haleakala. Having finally been discovered, the press had converged on the camp only to have Commander Jack Koehler, Executive Officer to Captain Ajax Couble, the base "C.O.", reveal that almost all of the UDTs were in the "forward areas". And now, the main job of those few men and officers remaining was to dismantled the base. And most particularly, to find a way to dispose of the thousands of tons of all types of military explosives. Today there is nothing left remaining to exactly pinpoint those facilities. Having been directed to one of the citizens of the Island best known for his knowledge of Maui's history, David Cup Choy could tell me nothing about the former base. Many of the older residents could write "chapter and verse" on the Fourth Marine Division. But had no knowledge of the UDTs and their base of tents. Never even knew it existed!

In the final build up, in anticipation of the operations against the Japanese home islands in October or early November, at that point twenty teams had finally been commissioned.

The war over.., and the Maui base suddenly no longer secret and "off limits", the Navy quickly assumed the role of good neighbor to the Island's "Parks and Playgrounds" commission.

With barges loaded with all types of UDT explosives at their disposal, the base had answered the call to clear coral reefs at the Island's Kalama Park.

Directed by Lieutenant Commander Tom Crist, a platoon of UDTs commanded by Ensign W.L. Hawkes blasted out the unwanted coral heads.

Blasting three times..., the UDTs cleared an area 100 yards by 300 yards. The Maui officials were intending to acquire the site for a new beach park. Never anticipating the growth in tourist traffic that has since transpired, at the time, there were numerous opposing protestors that claimed there were already more beaches set aside on the island than would ever be required to serve the public.

At the same time the island officials were arguing over the public beach issue, it is interesting to note that, they approved the purchase of the old Maxawao Japanese language school property for a "play center".

And down in Florida, at Fort Pierce, the original "Amphib" base of temporary buildings and tents was being rapidly dismantled by the UDT staff and a few remaining trainees. And by the early 1950s, the old South island "base area", where the NCDU and UDT camps had been located, would be developed into houses, motels, restaurants, etc. . The Navy Dispensary still survives as a motel. While the old Coast Guard Station has become a museum and historical landmark, a new Coast Guard Station had been constructed on the site of the Navy's "small boat" basin.

And in place of the officer's sleeping tents, located across from the officer's mess tent, is a building with an address of 1640 Seaway Drive, Fort Pierce, Florida, 34949. Now countless people enjoy the waterfront restaurant and Mangrove Matties Caesars Salads and seafood. And particularly the same view, of the Indian River and the Atlantic Ocean, that the UDTs saw from their old tent site over a half century earlier.

And back in California... , at Coronado... , several of the operational twenty teams had arrived from the "forward areas" in time for Navy Day... , 1945. And, at an impressive private UDT observance, the then Commander of the UDTs presented awards and medals and addressed those men and officers on hand for the ceremony on that date.

Unable to assemble all of the teams in one location on Navy Day 1945, each UDT returning to the states was presented with a copy of that address. And, after disembarking from their APDs, upon reporting to the new Coronado UDT Base, each team was commended by the UDT "CO", Captain R.H. Rodgers, USN, Commander Underwater Demolition Teams. The complete Navy Day, 1945, address of Captain Rodgers is provided in full as follows:

NAVY DAY SPEECH

Twenty Underwater Demolition Teams had taken part in the landings and occupation of Japan, Korea and China. Most, on operations or at sea on Navy day 1945, they were not present at the ceremony in which Captain R. H. Rodgers made the below address and the presentation of decorations.

"The Underwater Demolition Teams have played a part, little publicized, in this successful WWII. This policy was adopted in order to safeguard future operations against the enemy. With the conclusion of the peace the reason for the secrecy no longer exists."

OFFICE OF THE COMMANDER
UNDERWATER DEMOLITION TEAMS
and
UNDERWATER DEMOLITION FLOTILLA
AMPHIBIOUS FORCES, PACIFIC FLEET
San Francisco, Calif.

ADDRESS ON THE PRESENTATION OF MEDALS AT AMPHIBIOUS TRAINING BASE CORONADO ON NAVY DAY BY CAPTAIN R.H. RODGERS, COMMANDER UNDERWATER DEMOLITION TEAMS, AMPHIBIOUS FORCES, PACIFIC FLEET TO MEMBERS OF VARIOUS UNDERWATER DEMOLITION TEAMS FOR GALLANTRY IN ACTION AGAINST THE ENEMY.

It is with a feeling of intense pride that I (as the representative and in the name of the President of the United States) have the honor of bestowing upon members of these heroic teams here represented; and the grateful acknowledgment of the nation, to those honored. Medals are being presented to members of those first small demolition units who so bravely made possible the landing of our troops on the beaches of Normandy. Medals are being presented to those teams, who by their heroic action in the Marianas made possible the defeat of Japan. Medals are being presented to members of the Underwater Demolition Teams who far beyond the call of duty performed feats of heroism on board the U.S.S. Blessman (when that vessel was hit by a bomb) and, who by their heroic action quenched the fires on that vessel at Iwo Jima. Medals are being presented to the gallant men of those teams who for five days worked under enemy guns, on the beaches, and in the water, clearing the path that allowed our troops to land on Balikpapan.

Medals have been presented, previously, to other members of Underwater Demolition Teams assembled here. Medals will be presented when they arrive, to members of teams here and to the teams who have not yet returned to the United States. Some members will not receive medals. This does not mean that they did not perform equally heroic deeds but that recognition was not made.

The Underwater Demolition Teams have played a part, little publicized, in this successful WWII. This policy was adopted in order to safeguard future operations against the enemy. With the conclusion of the peace, the reason for the secrecy no longer exists. It was my hope that your part in this war will be increasingly recognized. I am sure that both your friends, and your family, can be justifiably proud of the great part that you have played in the war. No major amphibious assault was made without the Underwater Demolition Teams going in several days prior to D-Day. In this.., you were ably supported by the guns and aircraft of the Fleet. After making careful reconnaissance, you destroyed all underwater obstructions that would in any way impede the landing of troops. In spite of the fanatic enemy, the hazard of the sea, the heavy surf and the rough coral reefs, these teams never failed in any instance to fully accomplish their assignment from Kwajalein to Japan by way of Saipan, Iwo Jima, Okinawa, Balikpapen and all the other stepping stones. These teams have left a record of courageous service unsurpassed by any other organization. From a beginning of "small units", this organization grew until at the end of the war, there were 30 teams embarked on ships which composed the "Underwater Demolition Flotilla". Even after the completion of hostilities, it was necessary that 20 Underwater Demolition Teams be employed to accomplish the occupation of Korea, Japan and China.

You men, all "volunteers", were assisted by no secret weapon or equipment. You performed your duties with the courage, determination, loyalty of the American Bluejacket. On this first peaceful Navy Day for years, I congratulate you all with particular emphasis on those who are about to be decorated.

s/ R.H. Rodgers
R. H. RODGERS
CAPTAIN, U.S.N.

CHAPTER XIII.

A Man Returned From Hell

"A sailor's liberty is but for a day; yet while it lasts it is perfect."
R.H. Dana Jr.: "Two Years Before the Mast", xvi, 1940

With General Douglas MacArthur, and the occupation forces fully entrenched throughout the Japanese Islands, by the Spring of 1946, the powerful Third Fleet had been dispersed to many ports in the USA. And beginning a massive cleanup, the Navy had begun to accept the old Yamamoto headquarters at Yokosuka for it's far East base of operations.

But the lull in the far Pacific, heightened by nostalgic reports from "stateside", had caused a rapidly growing entourage of hostile elements among Third Fleet veterans. Sailors looking to return to the surroundings and men with whom they had grown comfortable.

Old Halsey sailors, cashing in all of their "chips", were lining up to join a similar old friend, Admiral Marc Andrew Mitscher, the announced "skipper' of the Navy's newly forming Eighth Fleet. Out of the Norfolk Operating Base, when Mitscher was named the new fleet's skipper, actually it did not even exist!

The crusty old early aviator is best remembered by old Navy hands for commanding the carrier Hornet at the battle of Midway, when the raiding U.S. planes were returning in the dark to a "blacked out" carrier deck. With none of his pilots qualified in night carrier landings, he recognized that they could not possibly spot the carrier's deck and land safely. His momentous order to turn on the landing lights, a heretofore unheard of decision to "light up the fleet", and when he replied to a cautionary warning, "there must be subs out there" with a quickly returned retort, "the hell with the subs!", earned him a legendary place in U.S. Naval History. And with that final decisive order, the wiry and gutsy old sailor won the hearts of every Naval aviator and sailor in the fleet.

But on March 1st, 1946, the same day that he had been promoted to a full four star Admiral, Mitscher broke out his Admiral's four star flag on the carrier U.S.S. Champlain, based at NOB, Norfolk. For his shore headquarters, he chose a very ordinary suite of offices in the base's administration building. While his new Eighth Fleet was "revving up" for a major deployment off the coast, the new Chief of Naval Operations, Admiral

Nimitz, was arranging for the Secretary of the Navy, James Forrestal and President Harry S. Truman to witness the new fleet on maneuvers. With the Washington "brass" as his guests, Mitscher arranged to transfer his flag to the carrier Franklin D. Roosevelt for those days at sea with the Secretary and the President. And it was the first time that a President of the United States had ever been aboard a carrier at sea. According to eye witnesses, the President, when not observing the fleet maneuvers, relaxed, played a lot of poker, and ate a lot of eggs while enjoying a few days of the sea air.

Anxious to join the old "task force" skipper from the Third fleet, sailors were pouring into Norfolk from all over the world. And, at the same time, ships from the "seven seas" were sent to decommission at the big operating base and to be stored temporarily until their disposition could be determined. In various moods of impatience, the crews waited to be relieved of duty along with many others also attached to ships critically short of personnel.

Norfolk had become alive with more activity than it had seen even in the height of the war. It was acknowledged that on many nights there were over 100.000 sailors trying to "pitch a little liberty" in downtown Norfolk... , mainly on Granby Street and Monticello Avenue.

Blood curdling bar brawls became a nightly occurrence... , they were almost commonplace. And caused a battery of corpsmen in the downtown Norfolk Court Street headquarters of the Shore Patrol to apply a monumental number of splints and bandages. Often working throughout the night. Bringing their young sons to the Court Street cell block, high ranking Naval Officers would take them into the cell area to see the mayhem resulting from overindulgence on a Saturday night liberty! And for a while, Norfolk gained a reputation for being another bloody beachhead. For war hardened sailors...., seeking a respite from the unaccustomed tranquility suddenly thrust upon them... , Norfolk was where the action was!

FIFTH NAVAL DISTRICT
U. S. NAVAL SHORE PATROL
236 Court Street
Norfolk, Virginia

In reply, Refer to

Telephone Norfolk 54581'

"A MAN RETURNED FROM HELL"

Three friends were sitting round the bar
Each one smoking a big black cigar
Each one guzzling down a beer
Each ones eyes filled with fear
Each one decided to go to war
To keep the japs from his door
But each one by some earthly chance
Had joined a different fighting branch.

Th Marine rose on wobbly feet
His eyes filled with much conceit
When this wars over we'll meet again
And I'll tell you stories of real fighting men
The soldier smiled, "you guys will learn
When you hear from me on my return"
The sailor didn't say a word
"I'll never brag or boast my men
Until I'm sure I'm back again."

And then they made a farewell bet
One that they would never forget
The one whose story was the best
The beers were paid for by the rest
The war was over and they were back
Drinking beer in the same old shack
The Marine with ribbons on his chest
Rose to his feet before the rest
"I saw action in the far South Seas
I shot Japs right out of the trees
Downed them like a bunch of fleas
Now beat that 'Dog Face", if you please."

And the soldier rose with a big smile
And laughed at the Marine for a while
"Friends I really saw the fight
In Italy, England and the Reich
I killed the Germans to my delight
But you would loose your appetite
If I told you of my every fight."

The sailor didn't say a word
And looked as if he hadn't heard
Then he hit the bar with an awful bruise
Said, "I was in Norfolk and Newport News"
The Marine jumped up and the soldier too
"Brother we owe drinks to you"
For each had heard and knew too well
There sat a man returned from HELL!!!!!

"Sailors … the world over, mourn the Passing of 'The
Krazy Kat"; headline in Norfolk newspaper, Summer 1960.

CHAPTER XIV.

1 JANUARY 1944

UNIVERSITY OF PENNSYLVANIA
U.S. NAVY V-12 UNIT

"A" COMPANY: 3rd PLATOON

Abbott, W.A.
Abrahamson, M.
Allinger, A.E.
Arn, J.
Cundiff, J.C.
Delman, R.J.
Fischer, R.L.
Gorski, F.I.
Hamilton, R.B.
Hammerschmidt, F.R.
Halkett, F.A.
Henderson, R.E.
Higgins, J.M.
Hirst, W.
Hoffman, H.S.
Hurst, T.J.
Harter, F.A.

James, L.A.
Koelsch, P.T.
Langstroth, W.T.
Leatherman, W.K.
Wiskind, M.I.
McGrath, J.A.
Matthews, R.A.
Morrow, W.C.
Muth, J.T.
Novak, S.
Ray, F.G.
Reynolds, R.A.
Seipp, H.E.
Tabachnick,N.
Taylor, C.E.
Tyma, J.H.
Williams, J.B.